COCKLESHELL
COMMANDO

COCKLESHELL
COMMANDO

by

BILL SPARKS
DSM

LEO COOPER

First published in Great Britain in 2002, reprinted in 2009 by
Pen & Sword Maritime
An imprint of
Pen & Sword Books Ltd
47 Church Street
Barnsley
South Yorkshire
S70 2AS

ISBN 978 184415 894 2

A CIP catalogue record for this book is
available from the British Library

Printed and bound in England
By CPI

Pen & Sword Books Ltd incorporates the Imprints of Pen & Sword Aviation,
Pen & Sword Family History, Pen & Sword Maritime, Pen & Sword Military,
Wharncliffe Local History,
Pen & Sword Select, Pen & Sword Military Classics, Leo Cooper, Remember
When, Seaforth Publishing and Frontline Publishing

For a complete list of Pen & Sword titles please contact
PEN & SWORD BOOKS LIMITED
47 Church Street, Barnsley, South Yorkshire, S70 2AS, England
E-mail: enquiries@pen-and-sword.co.uk
Website: www.pen-and-sword.co.uk

With Love
to
Irene

Also with sincere gratitude to my dear friend Jim Ruston,
without whose untiring efforts and patience in transcribing
my copious notes, this book may never have reached
the publisher.

Contents

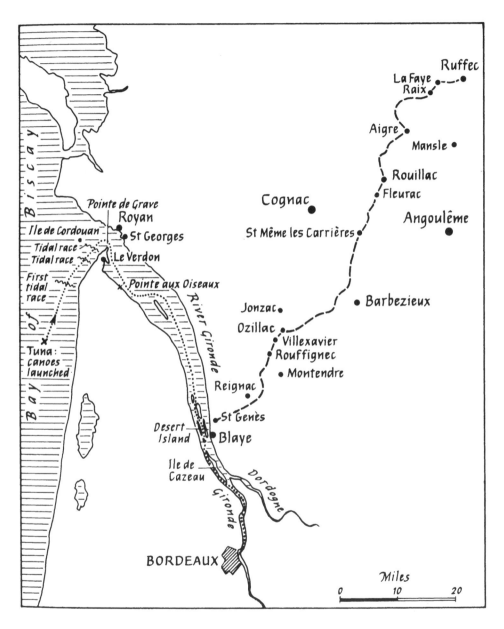

Operation Frankton

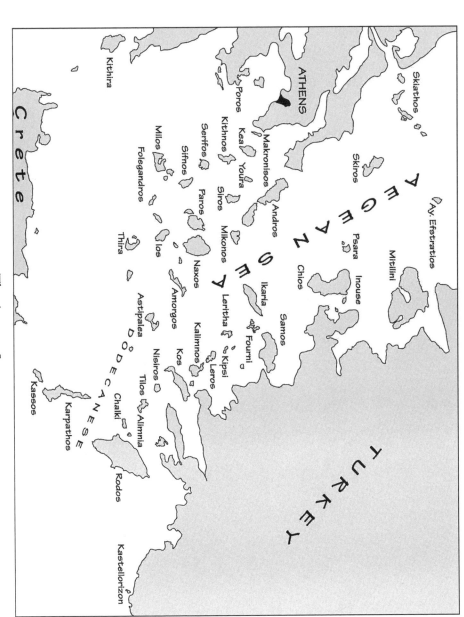

The Aegean Sea

Chapter 1

The Raid on Bordeaux

'Dear Mum Dad and brothers,

I'm taking this opportunity to write you these few lines, although I hope they won't be necessary. As you know I volunteered for a certain job, which I trust you will learn about at a later period. I've enjoyed every minute of it and hope that what we have done helps to end the mess we are in and make a decent and better world. You will see by recovery [sic] note whether I am a prisoner or otherwise, which at present isn't worrying me in the least. I have a feeling I'll be like a bad penny, so please don't upset yourself over my safety. My heart will be with you always, you are the best parents one could wish to have. Anyway Mum you can always say you had a son in the most senior service, and, though I say it myself, "one of twelve heroes".'

These moving words were written by Jock Ewart in a letter to his parents as we sat on board our 'hotel ship' *Al Rawdah* in the Clyde. There had not been room for us on the depot ship, so we had been accommodated on this old tug. The evening before we were to embark upon an 'exercise' of a secret nature, it was suggested we write a letter home. The twelve marines in the party were Major 'Blondie' Hasler, Lieutenant Mackinnon, Sergeant 'Mick' Wallace, Corporals Laver and Sheard, and Marines Conway, Mills, Moffat, Fisher, Ellery, Ewart and me – Bill Sparks – also known to my shipmates as Ned.

For the previous three months we had been training extensively for an operation of a 'particularly hazardous' nature. Our training indicated that it had something to do with blowing up ships, but

1

just when and where remained pure speculation. Now, it was rumoured, we were about to find out.

At first light on 30 November 1942 our six canoes with their respective names *Catfish*, *Coalfish*, *Cuttlefish*, *Crayfish*, *Conger* and *Cachalot* painted in small letters on their bows, were loaded aboard the submarine *Tuna*, which was moored alongside the depot ship HMS *Forth*. Reunited with our canoes, and in true 'Royal' fashion, following big ship tradition, as *Tuna* slipped her moorings, we stood to attention on the after casing, as the submarine saluted her depot ship. 'Carry On', shrilled out from the bo's'n's pipe, and we were dismissed and sent below, as the submarine glided down the Firth of Clyde, heading for open waters.

Now that the hatches had been closed and the ship was underway, Major Hasler called us all together. He had erected a blackboard in the forward torpedo space amongst our folded canoes and stores, and as we squatted close together he spoke. 'Right lads. This is it. The real thing.' He then drew a map of the Gironde estuary on the blackboard. As he did so, he explained that we were to be launched from our submarine under cover of darkness, at a place about ten miles from the headland named Pointe de Grave. From there we would paddle our canoes on a bearing that would take us to the mouth of the Gironde and then paddle a further sixty miles to Bordeaux where we were to do some 'business'. The raid, Major Hasler informed us, had a codename – Operation Frankton.

Well, I for one was completely taken by surprise. I had thought, as did the rest I suppose, that we were going after the German battleship *Tirpitz*, which was lying off the coast of Norway. Major Hasler continued to brief us on the job in hand. We were to paddle by night and lie up during the hours of daylight. The banks of the river were mostly covered in heavy reeds, ideal for concealment. But where there are reeds there is usually a lot of soft mud. This would have to be negotiated both when lying-up and again when re-launching – both times in total darkness.

There would also be another hazard, the Enemy! The defences were quite formidable. Apart from shore batteries, there were two armed trawlers on permanent patrol, six minesweepers, up to twelve torpedo boats plus another twelve patrol boats. Enemy U-boats could also be operating in the area. Besides all this there was the danger of being spotted from the air – the Germans had aerodromes at Bordeaux, Hourtain and Royan. A further threat of detection could come from the searchlight battery at Pointe de la Negade, to which we would have to pass very close. With a steely look in his eyes Major Hasler said, 'So you will all have to keep your eyes and ears peeled, and in daylight lie as low as possible.' He then continued to inform us that the point of the raid was to sink up to twelve merchant ships in the Bassens-Bordeaux area if possible, by placing magnetic limpet mines below the waterline on the stern and bow of the ships. Now it all became clear. During the past few weeks in Scotland we had done little else except to practice attacks on shipping in this very way.

Hasler looked around us then asked, 'Any questions so far?' Mick Wallace voiced the question that I am sure was on everyone's mind – it was definitely uppermost in mine. 'How do we get back sir?' 'I was coming to that next,' the officer answered. 'We must all appreciate that we cannot expect the submarine to come back to collect us, it will be at the very least eight days before we could possibly rendezvous with her, and our navigation isn't anything like good enough to make contact with her in the dark at sea. Plus of course, once our limpets have gone off there will be quite a few people looking for us! For this reason we will make our escape overland. After the attack we will paddle back down the estuary on the ebb tide, independently, getting as far as possible from Bordeaux as we can. Then land at low water, scuttle our boats, and make our escape through Spain and back to the UK. Each of you will have a specially prepared escape kit containing a map of your objectives, and the French resistance have been alerted to look out for us.'

Well you could have knocked me down with a feather. Yes, I was keen to have a crack at the enemy, but I hadn't bargained for this challenge. Looking about me I exchanged a few nervous grins with the others. We were not in any way prepared for this one; no one had mentioned the likelihood of it. After a few minutes it began to sink in, and a feeling of 'in for a penny, in for a pound' swept over me. Someone broke the ice with, 'How will we manage with the language sir. I can't speak a word of French?' 'Ah – well during the next couple of nights we shall have to swot up on a few phrases.'

During the first two days as *Tuna* proceeded down the Irish Sea and Bristol Channel a Force 4 wind was blowing causing the submarine to roll and making many of the men seasick. Thereafter we dived during daylight, coming to the surface at night to recharge the batteries and enjoy a most welcome intake of fresh air. It takes a while to get used to the claustrophobic conditions experienced in a submarine. Some never get used to it; and the feeling of nausea is exacerbated by the ever-lingering smell of diesel oil.

At 13.40 hours on 6 December Dick Raikes, the *Tuna*'s skipper, raised her periscope and announced that the French coast was now in sight. A wave of excitement coursed through the raiding party and anxious to get on with the job in hand we began making last minute checks on all of our gear. A while later Hasler told us there would be a delay in launching which caused a bit of an anti-climax. The reason for this he said was due to the submarine commander being unable to get a decent enough fix on our position. Captain Raikes informed Major Hasler that it was imperative to be dead accurate. He was also concerned about a minefield in the vicinity, which had been laid by our own Royal Air Force. 'I don't think those mines could possibly have been laid in a more embarrassing position,' he said. Finally getting the fix he needed, Raikes announced, much to the delight of Hasler, that he could put us down exactly where our commanding officer had requested. So it wasn't until early the next morning, with the sea flat calm, and under a starry sky, and with *Tuna* right inshore, that our mission began.

The method of launching the canoes was quite ingenious. A steel girder was fitted to the submarine's gun, to form an extension of it. Then a sling was attached from the gun's barrel to the canoe. Then complete with stores and two men aboard, the canoe was swung, using the gun's mechanism, over the casing of the submarine and into the water.

During briefing we were told that we would operate in two divisions made up thus:

A Division:
Hasler and Sparks *Catfish* Laver and Mills *Crayfish* Sheard and Moffat *Conger*

B Division:
Mackinnon and Conway *Cuttlefish* Wallace and Ewart *Coalfish* Ellery and Fisher *Cachalot*.

The target areas were: Bordeaux west bank; east bank; Bassens; north & south quays.

Once inside Bordeaux harbour we were to attack four of the largest cargo ships in there. These boats were being used to ferry large quantities of vital stores to help keep the mighty German war machine rolling. But with luck, we would stop them. A Div would place two limpets on each ship one amidships and one between there and the upstream end, five feet below the water line. B Div would do likewise on the downstream portion of the ship. This would give blanket coverage of the target area even if as expected, we did not all arrive on target at the same time.

During the last few days Hasler had impressed upon each and every one of us the importance of the mission, saying, 'Nothing must to be done to prevent us, or at least some of us from getting through. Any boat that gets separated from the rest must continue alone. Any boat that gets into difficulties and gives the SOS will only be aided by boats of its own division. Any canoe that gets swamped and cannot be bailed out will be scuttled and its crew left to swim for it with their No. 5 bags [these contained dry clothes and escape kit]. Never take offensive action unless compelled. Your job is to get through. If you are challenged or fired upon, adopt the lowest position and let the tide carry you. Never return fire. If you have to, kill silently with your fighting knife. If you are unfortunate enough to be captured there is a secret system by which you may be able to send a message back to England giving useful information. Lieutenant Mackinnon will brief you on this. Practise it among yourselves.'

About 19.30 hours the submarine surfaced. Below, we of the raiding party had re-built our canoes, checked our kit, and had our last meal on the submarine and waited in readiness. 'Up Canoes.' It was Raikes's voice coming down the voice-pipe. The forehatch was opened and the hoisting party, made up of submariners, went into action. First the tackle for securing the submarine's gun appeared, then came the boats. *Catfish* was up last so as to be first on the hoist out. With our faces blacked up and carrying our personal weapons, which included a silent Sten gun, we mustered on deck. However, not all went smoothly. As *Cachalot* came up through the hatch she was snagged along her canvas wall, thus rendering her un-seaworthy. 'I'm afraid you will have to stay behind,' Hasler informed Marines Fisher and Ellery. The two men were devastated, to the point that Eric Fisher shed tears. I felt immense compassion for them. To have come this far . . . Thirty minutes later, the rest of us were water-borne and in formation. The ship's company of *Tuna* waved *au revoir* (Captain Raikes own words) 'to a magnificent bunch of black-faced villains, with whom it had been a pleasure to work.'

In arrowhead formation with B Div astern of us (with one barb missing) Hasler and I paddled along in silence. Due to the load they were carrying, the canoes rode low in the water. Ours was leaking a bit, so I had to bail it out often. The seawater was freezing and there was an icy wind. To add to my misery the spray from Hasler's paddle was striking me in the face, making my eyes smart. After a while Hasler gave the signal for the others to close on him, and we rafted up. Everyone was in good spirits, and reported all well, although Sergeant Mick Wallace had been heard throwing up. The light was good and we could see each other clearly, and chatted away for a good few minutes. We set off again, paddling strongly. The strong flood tide was now being felt, so we altered course – slightly more eastward, to follow the line of the coast that was now clearly visible. I could hear a roaring sound ahead of us, and wondered what it was. Hasler again gave the signal to raft up. Once we were all together he explained what it was we could now all clearly hear. 'We are coming to a tidal race. There is nothing to be alarmed about, all you have to do is to remember your rough-water drill and, once you get through, raft up again.' I gulped, but took comfort in the knowledge, that the man I was paddling behind, was probably the best canoeist in the world.

We proceeded in the direction of the roar. As we got nearer I could see the white foaming surf; against a black sky it looked awesome. The tide was carrying us along at a fair old pace, so before I had time to worry any more we were in swirling waters, and being thrown around like a cork. I dug deep, using every ounce of strength, conscious of the need to keep the canoe balanced, and struck ahead. Suddenly, we were in calm waters once more. We swung our canoe about and watched for the others to come through. The first to appear was *Crayfish*, then *Conger* and finally *Cuttlefish*. But where was *Coalfish* with Mick Wallace and Jock Ewart? Hasler ordered everyone to search for the missing canoe. We scanned the inky waters but could see nothing. I sounded the seagull alarm – we each carried one for identification purposes – but there was no response. If *Coalfish* had capsized, her buoyancy bags would keep her afloat and she should still come through.

Likewise, Mick and Jock were wearing lifejackets, so they should be able to swim on. We waited. After what seemed like an eternity, now soaked and chilled to the marrow, and with the tide pushing us away from the tide-race, Hasler said that we must press on. The fate of Wallace and Ewart is revealed in a much later chapter.

So it was with great concern for our mates that the remainder of us paddled on into the unknown. Already we had lost one third of our raiding force. We were now travelling at a cracking pace, helped considerably by the flood tide and a renewed determination to see this thing through. I was taking it all very personally. No way would I let my mates Mick and Jock down. (Later it transpired that in fact we never let each other down).

The lighthouse on the Pointe de Grave became visible and we passed between it and the island of Cordouan which was in darkness. Hasler was visibly pleased because it meant that his navigation had been spot-on and we were now approaching the entrance to the Gironde estuary. Then to my dismay, I could hear once more that awesome roaring sound, only this time it was even louder. We braced ourselves and with our cockpit canopies drawn up tight and every sinew of muscle tense, we paddled without hesitation into the swirling waters. This was much worse than before. The waves must have been at least five feet high, and we were tossed around like a toy boat. There was a shout and a splash and *Conger* capsized. Its crew, Corporal Sheard and Marine Moffat were now in the water.

Somehow, the two marines managed to hang on to their canoe, eventually coming through the swirling waters. The sea was so cold that ice had begun to form on the bows of our canoe. So just what it was like for our poor mates, who were now swimming in it, God alone knew? Hasler gave the order for us to raft up so that he could examine *Conger,* to see if she could be re-floated but it was hopeless. Hasler told the forlorn marines to hang on to a canoe each, then gave me the order to scuttle *Conger.* This was easier said than done. The tide was pushing us all along with some ferocity, and the canvas sides of the canoe were extremely strong, so it took quite a bit of lunging and tearing away with my clasp knife before *Conger* slid under the water. Things were looking grim indeed, and to add to our anxiety, the revolving lighthouse on Pointe de Grave suddenly switched to full power. We were lit up like decorations on a Christmas tree. Time also was not on our side. We could not afford to linger, so Major Hasler made the agonizing decision to tow Sheard and Moffat as close to the shore as we dare, hoping they could swim the remaining distance alone. At this point, to say our hearts were heavy would be the understatement of the century. We paddled on.

The added weight, and excess drag, caused by the two comrades we were towing, made life very difficult indeed. Then, yet again, we could hear the formidable sound ahead – another bloody tide race. We entered the perilous waters with Sheard clinging on to our boat and Moffat hanging on to the canoe of Lieutenant Mackinnon. This time, the passage was less violent, so we came through unscathed. At last the tide carried us round the point from which the lighthouse was beaming down on us, and into the Gironde. Our thoughts were very much for the welfare of the two in the water. They had been immersed for over an hour and were bitterly cold. We also had to consider making for a suitable laying-up place.

Then, ahead of us we could just make out the outline of the pier of Le Verdon. The tide was sweeping us towards the pier, and with the extra weight and drag, there was little we could do to avoid it. Once more Hasler had to make an agonizing decision. He addressed the two marines in the water in a low voice, 'I'm afraid this is as far as we can take you. The tide should carry you close to the pier. Hopefully you can make it to the shore undetected. God bless you both.' The reply, which came from Corporal Sheard, was typical of him, 'That's all right, sir, it was good of you to take us this far.' Corporal Laver whipped out a small flask with rum in and stuffed it inside Sheard's jacket. The rum was a gift from the submariners – thank God for it – and them. I cannot describe how I felt at leaving my two mates in the water to fend for themselves; it was devastating.

We were paddling south against a strong current, and could now see beyond the pier head. There in the distance was the outline of four ships, similar in shape and size to destroyers; we would have to pass between them and the Verdon jetty, which would almost certainly be patrolled by sentries. Once again we closed up for instructions. In a voice barely above a whisper Hasler told us 'We will have to go single file, one canoe at a time, in the single-paddle low-profile mode until we are clear. Sparks and I will go first. Corporal Laver, when you see that we are clear, follow us. Mac, you follow *Crayfish*.' This last instruction was addressed to Lieutenant Mackinnon.

Hasler and I set off. Paddling gently, and bent over our canoe, we drifted through the channel between the ships and the jetty. My back felt naked; I could see a light flickering ashore and thought it must be pointing at us. However, no call or shot came and soon we were through and into the darkness beyond. After a few minutes we could see the outline of *Crayfish*, and soon Laver and Mills were by our side. Now we waited for Mackinnon and *Cuttlefish*. We waited and waited but still there was no of sign of them. We thought we heard something – I thought it was probably a sentry. Then all was quiet again. By now I was freezing and could hardly feel my hands as they gripped the paddle. The woollen gloves we all wore were now so wet they offered no protection against the cold. I felt thoroughly miserable and not a little downhearted. What had happened to our second in command, and his No. 2, Marine Conway? Again I sounded my seagull cry. There was no reply.

It was around 06.00 hours and we were running out of time before first light. Just as dawn was breaking we found a small sandy projection called Pointe aux Oiseaux. Hasler stepped out of our canoe and made a quick reconnaissance – a one hundred yard sweep. After satisfying himself that it was safe he signalled us to follow. It was agony to move a limb, let alone drag the canoes up the beach, but somehow we managed it. It wasn't the best of hiding places but it would have to do. It was a tired and hungry bunch that covered the canoes with camouflage nets, and started to sort out a hot drink and a meal from our compact rations.

I now wondered about our chances of success. It was a lot to ask of just four men with two canoes. I also pondered on the fate of those we had lost – praying to God that they were safe.

As dawn broke we could now see that we were close to the small creek that led to the tiny village of St Vivien. We could hear the chugging sound of small motor vessels making their way down the creek into the river. This didn't alarm us unduly, that is until we realized that some of the boats were turning back and making directly for the spot where we were hiding; then my stomach knotted a bit. We could hear the unmistakable sound of women chattering and what sounded like pots and pans clanging together. Soon, a number of men came up from the boats they had dragged onto the beach. Now men and women were talking noisily, and starting to make a fire. Surely they must have seen us? They were only a few yards away. Hasler decided that not to make contact might provoke all sorts of complications, and ordered us to cover him whilst he approached them. After a while Hasler returned saying he thought he had convinced them that we were English soldiers. But they had made no promises about not reporting what they had seen, only that they would discuss it between themselves. We could only stay low and hope.

All day we waited, taking it in turns to sleep whilst the others kept guard. It was just getting dark when one of our group cried, 'Look out! – Jerries.' We all turned, and seeing the shapes of about fifty men advancing towards us, we drew our weapons, and the major cocked his silent Sten gun. Marine Mills muttered, 'So the French have given us away after all.' We watched with a nervous tension that consumed our beings. Hasler raised his field glasses then said 'You can relax, they are not Jerries, just the same line of stakes that we have been looking at all day!' The tiredness and stress had caused us to hallucinate. We had to shake it off. 'Get some more sleep,' our leader ordered. 'It will be hours before we can leave here.' In fact we couldn't leave until about 23.30 hours when the flood tide would be running. Even then we would have to drag our laden canoes across the mud for about three-quarters of a mile.

It was no easy task getting our canoes afloat, but soon we were paddling furiously, which did help to get the blood flowing, although we were still frozen stiff.

We stopped every hour for a brief rest, ate some biscuits and when we felt it necessary, took a Benzedrine tablet. It has to be cold for seawater to freeze; that night it was freezing on the covers of the canoe's cockpit. Hasler checked our position on his chart and with the dim red light from his torch confirmed it with Corporal Laver. We were making really good time when as we crossed the shipping channel to the east side, we were nearly run down by a half-dozen ships. We had to paddle like mad to keep out of their way.

We picked up the east bank north of Port des Callonges and kept the shoreline in sight until dawn was about to break. We put in to shore and found a suitable spot to alight from our canoes. The water ran right up to the edge of a field where we were able to step from the canoes onto land. We found an excellent place to hide, in

10

a dry ditch, between two hedges. Exhausted, we brewed tea, and got some rations down us. Then, without encouragement, took it in turns to sleep soundly under a pale blue winter sky. The only disturbance was when an aircraft swept low over our position; so low in fact that we could see the pilot clearly in the cockpit. Also a few hundred yards away there was a farmhouse. But as we could see no activity in its vicinity we shrugged it off. We had made up most of the time we had lost, and this gave us heart.

Reluctantly, we prepared to leave our safe hiding place in the evening, but as we did so, a Frenchman came running towards us. He followed us down to the bank and watched as we launched our canoes. The major engaged him in conversation telling him we were Englishmen, and that would he please not give us away. The Frenchman then implored us all to go to his house for a drink. Explaining that 'thank you, but we cannot accept your offer – perhaps another time' we climbed into our canoes. The French farmer assured us he would say nothing; nevertheless it unnerved us.

We now had to negotiate the many islands that lay further up the estuary and no doubt more marine activity. We were making good progress when out of nowhere came the heavy throbbing of a motorboat. We darted in amongst some thick reeds on the edge of the water, and watched silently as the launch sped by. With the coast clear we made our exit from the reeds and paddled strongly, but not without caution, towards the island, which Major Hasler had picked and codenamed Desert Island – our next lying-up place. Although we had only been paddling for a few hours, it was necessary to get out of the water whilst the tide changed. At evening twilight with visibility too good for comfort we emerged from our hide. In due time we reached the banks of Desert Island, its banks were covered in dense reeds that made a loud crackle as we attempted to penetrate them. With perseverance we eventually got our canoes and ourselves ashore and into a small clearing.

Next morning we got plastered in icy mud lifting and sliding our canoes across the beach. It took a great deal out of us, and brought on a muck sweat, which when cold added to our already considerable discomfort. Now with the banks close on either side, and in single paddle order, we proceeded with extreme caution. These were very dangerous waters. Before first light we approached the southern end of the Île Cazeau and began to look for a likely hiding

11

place. After some considerable time Hasler went ashore to reconnoitre. Soon he returned saying he had come across a gun emplacement, so it would be too risky to alight here. We continued upstream to where the island came to a sort of point, and landed there. The sky was lightening by the minute as we carried our canoes into the middle of some dense grass, set them down, erected our camouflage nets, and climbed in.

Still freezing cold we sat stock still in our boats. Silence was of the essence. We could not brew up or smoke because only a few trees separated us from the gun emplacement. We were like a fly in a spider's web hoping that the spider would not return. If only we could have known, on this very same island, but a few miles from where we hid, Mackinnon and Conway were themselves in hiding. To add to our anxiety aircraft were flying low overhead, and a small herd of cows was coming our way. We were now in the waters of the Garonne – Bordeaux was just twelve miles away. Even so, Major Hasler confided in us that he thought we were still too far away from our target and wanted to move closer before preparing to strike. None of us was sorry to leave this island; our movements had been far more restricted here than anywhere so far. We could have done with a little more sleep though. All we had managed during the hours of daylight, was the odd catnap. Close to 19.00 hours, with a creaking of bones and tired bodies, we carried our canoes to the water's edge and launched them.

There was a drop of rain and it was much darker than it had been, so conditions for concealment were far better. Paddling steadily with double scull, we kept to the centre of the river, then, after a couple of miles, changed to single paddles and hugged the riverbank. We rounded a bend in the river and at once could see two ships moored at the quayside on the opposite bank to the one we had been following, at what we reckoned must be Bassens south. This brought us up sharp with the feeling that 'at last' we had arrived at one of our targets.

Nearby on our own side there was a small pontoon. We ducked as we slid noiselessly underneath it and out the other side. Now we searched for somewhere to lie up. This was easier to find than we had expected. The riverbank was dense with tall reeds, some more than eight feet high. We found a small rivulet and pushed our way in as deep as we could. Here we settled and waited for first light in anticipation of what we might be able to observe.

With the dawn came a hubbub of activity. Sounds of people going about their work were all around. The noisy cranes on the quay were swinging their jibs to and fro unloading cargo. There was that much row, we were able to talk quietly without fear of being overheard.

The tide had ebbed, so our canoes were sat on the mud. The sturdy construction of the flat-bottomed craft allowed us to stand up, have a much-needed stretch, and a very welcome pee! It was 11 December and Major Hasler told us of his final plan for the attack. As I listened intently to the officer's instructions, with the adrenaline now pumping round my body at full speed, all the tiredness and pain seemed to lift from me. Hasler said we would wait until 21.00 hours before leaving our hide. This would enable us to float the three miles up river to Bordeaux on the flood, do the business and return downstream on the ebb as far as possible until the next flood tide prevented us from continuing; then land on the eastern bank, scuttle our canoes, and make our escape.

We checked our equipment thoroughly, putting everything we needed to assist us in our escape into two bags. Then it was time to fuse our limpet mines. We were told to fit orange ampoules, which would give around nine hours' delay. Whilst we armed the sixteen limpets Hasler watched over us like a hawk. We also checked that the placing rod connected and disconnected freely with each limpet. The last thing we needed was for the rod to get fouled up whilst attaching a limpet to the hull of a ship.

Major Hasler gave the order, 'Start your fuses.' We turned the thumbscrew of each limpet until we heard the click signalling that the glass ampoule had broken, releasing its penetrating agent. Now nothing would stop these mines going off in about nine hours' time. It's an odd feeling sitting with explosives between your legs. What if something went wrong with the ampoule? I didn't suppose we would know much about it, so why worry! I put it out of my mind. We slid our canoes through the reeds into the water, shook hands, wished each other luck, and went our separate ways.

The water was flat calm and we paddled under a clear night sky. To add to our concern about possible detection, the port was not blacked out, but lit-up like Oxford Street at Christmas. After just over an hour of paddling the targets came into view – lined up like sitting ducks at a fairground, a line of ships. Powerful lamps illuminated the decks of the vessels and spilled their light onto the water; more lamps flooded the lock entrance. We paddled in an arc, keeping on the edge of the lamps' beams. We were far enough out from our targets to see that there were seven ships for the picking or, should I say, sinking.

It was high water slack, the tide would soon ebb, and we had to get on with it. Keeping in the shadow of the hull of a big tanker, in low profile single paddle, we crept along until we came to a fat cargo ship. Hasler gave me the signal to clamp my magnetic hold-fast onto the side of the vessel to keep the canoe in position. He then fitted a limpet to the placing rod and lowered it under water as far as he could. Once the magnet on the mine had fixed itself to the hull of the ship, Hasler gently disengaged the rod and pulled it up. One down – seven to go! Stealthily we moved amidships, and this time, because the current was trying to swing the bows of the canoe out from the ship's side, we changed roles. Hasler now held on to the holdfast whilst I planted the mine. We stayed in this mode until I planted another mine close to the ship's stern. Three mines were now attached. We hoped it would be enough to do serious damage. We continued along the line until we came to the last ship in the group. It wasn't quite the type of vessel we wanted, but there was a *Sperrbrecher* (a warship about the size of a frigate) moored alongside and we thought her fair game. Again Hasler held *Catfish* against the side our victim, whilst I planted two limpets on her – no hard feelings, old girl!

It was time to turn about and go back downstream. To achieve this, we had to swing *Catfish* out from under the protection of the ship's hull, and as we did we heard the distinct sound of a pair of heavy boots on the deck above us. Suddenly we were caught in the beam of a powerful torch – we froze. Luckily we had just about managed to get *Catfish* back against the hull – and there we stayed. Hoping against hope that the sentry would mistake us for a piece of driftwood, we let the canoe drift gently on the ebb. We could hear the sentry walking back down the ship, as if following us. After what seemed like an eternity we were under the flare of the ship's bows. Hasler passed me the holdfast and motioned to me to clamp on. This I did as silently as possible. I thought, 'Now what.' We waited with baited breath hoping to hear the sound of the sentry's receding steps. None came. Then Hasler signalled me to unclamp, and in low profile with paddles shipped we let *Catfish* drift downstream on the tide.

14

Once we were clear, we decided to attack the big cargo ship we had passed earlier. She had a tanker moored alongside so we positioned *Catfish* between them. This almost caused a catastrophe. The strong ebb tide was causing a swell, which in turn pushed the two vessels together. We just managed to back paddle in time; another few seconds and we would have been crushed. What an end that would have been. We drifted further down the side of the tanker, and this time managed to get between the vessels safely, before planting two limpets, as far apart as we could, on the stern of the cargo ship.

Hasler turned around and grabbed me warmly by the hand. For the first time in days we had a smile on our faces. With that, we made for the middle of the river in order to take advantage of the strong current, and away we went. It was a miracle we were not spotted; we must have been clearly visible. My mind turned to home. Could we make it? We had been lucky thus far – was it too much to hope for? First we would have to get as far back down the estuary as tide and darkness would allow. With double paddles we fairly screamed along, and soon we were among the myriad islands. In midstream, we stopped for a rest and drifted. Then out of the blue we heard a familiar noise coming from behind us. First the sound of frantic paddling, then a seagull note. We responded, and soon we could see the outline of a canoe. It was *Crayfish* with Corporal Laver and Marine Mills. I could have cheered. We rafted up and they told us that they had attacked the two ships at Bassens South. 'Well done! Well done all of you. I am so proud of you.' Blondie's congratulations were warmly received and returned by all.

All too soon after our short reunion, Hasler beckoned it was time to go. At first he said we should split up then and there. But Laver asked if we could stay together a little longer; after some thought Hasler agreed, saying, 'Well all right, but we shall have to separate before we land.' United once more, we 'blacked-up villains', swept back down the Gironde. We had made it down the river to just north of St Genès-de-Blaye when the tide began to turn. We had travelled nintey-odd miles over five nights; Hasler signalled for the last time to raft-up. He told Laver and Mills to land, scuttle their canoe, and make their escape as planned. We would paddle a little further on before landing and following suit. We shook hands and wished each other the very best of luck. Pleased as I was to be on my way, I felt sad parting from my mates. As we paddled away, I called back, 'See you in Granada. We'll keep a couple of pints for you.' Then my thoughts turned to the rest of the lads. What had become of them? Tragically, that parting was to be the last I ever saw of any of them.

We put in to shore near the village of St Genès-de-Blaye, and pulled the canoe onto the soft mud. It was ecstasy to be out of the boat after nine hours of restricted movement. Every bone in my body cracked like a rifle shot. We removed the bags containing our escape kit which consisted of a silk handkerchief with a map etched onto it, several tiny luminous compasses (prone to failure if wet), some malted milk tablets and some book matches with the V-sign and manufacturer's name printed on them. The latter could hopefully serve to identify anyone who carried them as probably being English. This would help when making contact with the resistance. We also removed the last of our compact rations and a small can of fresh water. We carried all we needed up the slippery sloping shore, to the top of a mud bank on which tall reeds grew. We then returned to scuttle the canoe. It was like plunging a knife into a good friend, but it had to be done. Major Hasler waded out into the river pushing the semi-submerged canoe, until with one last push, she drifted away on the tide. I could just see the bows of *Catfish* poking above the water as she disappeared into the darkness.

It took quite some time to penetrate the reeds – the soft mud hindered us greatly. We stumbled against a low wire fence and then another and another. It was only after a few more that Hasler exclaimed, 'You know where we are, don't you Sparks? We're in a bloody vineyard.' I chuckled to myself, thinking what fools we were. But then in mitigation, answered, 'Well sir, it's difficult to see anything in this light.' It was an inky black night. The vines were to prove a constant nuisance to us. All we could do was zig-zag in and out of the lines. Looking at one of the little compasses, with its needle bobbing around, we took a bearing north-east. Soon we were walking briskly and beginning to dry out a little. As dawn approached, luckily, we came into a wood. We found a small stream and settled nearby, using the running water to drink and clean ourselves up a little.

Hasler looked at his watch and said it was 09.30 hours. I asked if he thought we might hear the limpets going off from where we were. He said he thought it extremely unlikely. 'It would be nice to hear them though.' I added. Soon tiredness overcame us and we were fast asleep. At first light and after a hot cup of tea we discussed our strategy. Being still in uniform, we would have to hide during daylight, and travel under the cover of darkness. It would take us about a week to reach Ruffec where we hoped to make contact with an escape organization.

That evening we came upon a small farmhouse and Hasler decided to take a chance and knock at the door. We desperately needed to get out of our uniforms and into civilian clothes. We also needed food. I watched from a distance as the door opened and the Major disappeared inside. A few minutes went by before he waved to me to me to join him. The farmer and his family looked decidedly nervous. I guessed they were taking an awful risk helping us. As I could not speak a word of French, Hasler translated telling me that there was no food to spare but there was some clothing on offer. We were given a pair of rough trousers each and in addition I was given an old poacher's coat. The farmer agreed to burn the uniforms we left, and still looking more than anxious, waved us away.

As we walked away looking as motley a couple of travelling companions as you are ever likely to encounter, Blondie said, 'Bill, now that we are in civilian clothes we will have to discard our weapons. If we are captured in civvies, and armed, we will be shot.' They say 'ignorance is bliss' for had we known then, that in fact the enemy not only knew our names, but also had our descriptions, it wouldn't have mattered what we were dressed in! I was reluctant, to say the least, to part with my pistol, fighting knife, and a grenade I had secreted about my person. But I did as I was bid and dug a hole with my knife then buried it with the rest of the weapons.

Had we known that there were Germans in St. Même-les-Carrières, we would have avoided it. However, relying on information we had been fed by our Intelligence, that it was unoccupied, we pushed boldly on, straight through the middle. We were passing a big old house when a door flew open and a group of rowdy German soldiers spilled out into the road – directly into our path. They literally walked right through between us, elbowing us out of their way as went. Cheeky sods! My pulse raced.

We continued through the village and out into open countryside.

After another agonizing hike we came to a remote farmhouse and knocked on the door, only to have it open then slam in our faces. The locals were definitely nervous of strangers. They had every right to be. It was a well-known fact that anyone assisting the enemies of Germany would be hauled off for interrogation, tortured, and probably executed. Why would anyone risk their life for a couple of unconvincing tramps? It was pouring with rain and we were miserable. Walking down a track we came across a barn into which we peered cautiously. We were starving, having eaten what few rations we had saved from the canoe, but all we could do was burrow our way into the soft sweet smelling hay.

We slipped into a deep slumber, and then suddenly something made me sit up. It was a strong light shining in my face. The beam was coming from a torch held by a French farmer. Without my weapons I felt defenceless. The major quickly assured the farmer that we were escaping British soldiers. 'It is too dangerous for you to be here. You are lucky I spotted you before someone else did. There are hostile people around these parts. You had better come into my house.' We followed him out into the rain, and along a track until we came to a farmhouse. Our host ushered us inside, where a good log fire was crackling away in the fireplace. 'Sit, sit.' the Frenchman insisted, then left the room. Soon he was back with soup and bread. What a welcome sight that was.

It was suggested we return to the barn for a few hours and leave well before first light. However, just as I was getting cosy, the farmer was flashing his torch in my face again and urging both of us to leave quickly. The rain beat down relentlessly as we scurried away from the barn. 'What was all that about sir,' I enquired. Major Hasler replied 'It seems someone spotted us earlier on and they've informed the gendarmes, who are on their way to investigate.' I quickened my pace! We slogged on. The journey seemed endless. It was 18 December and we walked all day until darkness enveloped us. Then we decided to chance our luck once more. We could see a house on the edge of a forest that looked pretty remote.

A young girl responded to our door knocking, and much to our surprise invited us in. Before we had chance to ask for anything a young man of about sixteen entered the house. Hasler explained that we were British commandos, and at once the lad said that, although he was not in a position to help us, he knew of those who

18

could. We had little choice but to follow this young man; if it was a trap we were done for. After walking for about half an hour we came to a clearing in which a small house was neatly tucked to one side of the path – almost obscured from view.

The lad led us into the house and there before us was the roughest bunch of villains I had seen for a long while. My heart sank. They said they were part of a *maquis* cell that was intent on killing Germans. I gulped, hoping we could convince them we were on their side. They started to interrogate Hasler. Then one of the Frenchman switched on a radio set. Hearing the voice of the English announcer distracted my attention; I was now hell bent on listening to every word he was saying. I didn't realize it but my reactions were being keenly observed. Suddenly the leader of the group exclaimed, 'Our brave English friends. They must be hungry. Get them some food, and wine.' It seemed, that for the moment at least, we were among allies.

We were shown to a huge double bed and slept like babes. Next morning with a hearty breakfast inside of us, and food and water that had been so kindly provided for the next part of our journey, we thanked our hosts most sincerely. Our young friend was beckoning us to follow him, saying also, 'By tomorrow we should be in Ruffec.' Those words were music to my ears. We walked until midday then stopped for a rest. To my surprise, and may I say delight, when I lifted my water can to drink, instead of the bland taste of water I had expected, my palate was awash with sweet red wine! Blondie was also smiling at discovering the contents of his can. We ate a little food then continued our hike. The wine was making our legs feel like lead, so when we came to a stream we refilled one of the cans with water. This helped to balance our intake of fluid and clear our heads a bit.

As night fell we found an old barn and crept inside. This time there was no hay, and to add to our discomfort it was verminous. But at least it was shelter from the elements. Next morning we cut across country. Trudging through puddles and mud, we passed through the village of Raix. The few people that were about seemed oblivious of our presence as the three of us ambled along. Our guide informed us that in fact Ruffec was now just three miles further on. A couple of miles later we came to the village of La Faye. We were on the road heading east. We had Ruffec in our sights, when our young companion announced that this was where he must leave us.

19

He wished us good luck, and before we could say more than 'thanks' he turned, and walked away briskly, retracing his tracks. What a brave young fellow.

Our instructions had been that, once in Ruffec, we were to go immediately to the Café de Paris. Walking the streets, looking for the café, we were acutely aware of our bedraggled appearance. Surely we would stand out? But try as we might we were unable to find the elusive Café de Paris. We had to take a chance so we went into a café we both thought looked unimposing, and sat down. The major had the menu in his hand when a waitress of ample proportions came over to our table. She said something to him that turned his face white. Apparently everything was rationed; we needed ration cards, even for a drink. However, on the menu was potato soup, for which coupons were not required. Hasler ordered two bowls. This we ate as slowly as possible to give us time to think. When we had finished the major whispered that he would order more and hopefully, if we could hang out here long enough without rousing suspicion, the resistance might find us. After all, they had been told to expect escaping commandos.

We waited and waited then Hasler took the initiative by calling the waitress over to pay the bill. In our escape kit we had 2,000 francs. Hasler wrote a small message in French on a piece of paper that read: 'We are escaping English soldiers. Do you know anyone who can help?' He wrapped it inside a 500 franc note and handed it to the lady. The Frenchwoman went back to her till and unravelled the note. She became animated and started clearing people from the café. When she disappeared through a rear door I thought, 'What if she turns us in?' But then, what were we to do? We just sat and waited our fate.

When the waitress returned she had a little old man in tow. To our surprise he spoke perfect English. Things were looking up. Or so I thought. Some conversation followed during which the little man asked pointed questions about what had led us here. It was a game of cat and mouse. The major needed to tell him sufficient to establish that we were genuine, but not more. The details of our mission we must keep to ourselves. After more questions the man said that, as much as he would have liked to, he could offer no help. A younger man came, but after more questions, conceded that he could not help us either. We were beginning to despair. Hasler asked madame if she had a room for the night, and she nodded and

20

C.R. 4451/43

COMBINED OPERATIONS HEADQUARTERS,
1A, RICHMOND TERRACE,
WHITEHALL, S.W.1.

Telephone :
WHitehall 9777

2nd July, 1943.

Dear Sparks,

I am delighted to see
that you have been awarded the
Distinguished Service Medal and
am writing to offer you my most
sincere congratulations.

This is the fitting
tribute to the courage and
resourcefulness that you showed
on your hazardous operation.

Yours sincerely,

Louis Mountbatten

1. The letter I received from Admiral
Lord Mountbatten, then Chief of
Combined Operations, after I was
awarded the DSM.

Army Form C 2127—
(In pads of 100

URGENT MEMORANDUM.

Reference No. MD/JAG/A/58

From Officer i/c Military Department,
The Judge Advocate General's Office,
6, Spring Gardens, London. S.W.1.

Date 13th August 1948

Subject T.D. BAOR.

To W.E. Sparks, Esq.,

1. You are hereby requested to proceed to Hamburg on
Monday 16th August 1948 to act as a witness at a War
Crimes Trial.

2. You should report to the R.T.O., Liverpool Street
Station at 1915 hours on the 16th August, ready in all
respects to board the Harwich/Hook route train which
leaves Liverpool Street at 2000 hours on that date.
From the Hook you will catch the train to Hamburg where
you will be met.

3. You will be allowed to take only £5. sterling out of
the country.

4. Railway warrant and embarkation papers for both out-
ward and return journeys are attached. The warrant for
your rail journeys on the other side will be issued by the
R.T.O. The Hook on presentation of this authority.

5. Please acknowledge receipt of these instructions on
one of the carbon copies; the others you will require en
route.

Staff Captain,
Military Department,
J.A.G's Office.

Signature.

20987. Wt.W8300/2732. 5,000 Pads. 11/47. K. & H., Ltd. G65766.

2. The summons I received to attend
the war crimes trials of those
responsible for murdering my
comrades.

---

3. My Malayan police handbook.

Copy No.

This handbook issued to

.T. W. E. SPARKS.

the property of the Federation of Malaya Police
rce and upon the termination of the services
the holder should be returned to Police
Headquarters, Kuala Lumpur.

THE FEDERATION OF MALAYA
POLICE FORCE

POLICE HANDBOOK

for the guidance of the

FEDERATION OF MALAYA
POLICE FORCE

All rights reserved

FOR USE OF POLICE ONLY

4. Photographed (1999) with the man (right) who as a teenager took me over the line of demarcation during my escape through France.

5. The identity disc taken from me by M. DuBois and returned at the French premier of the film *Cockleshell Heroes*.

6. The photograph used on my forged papers during our escape through France.

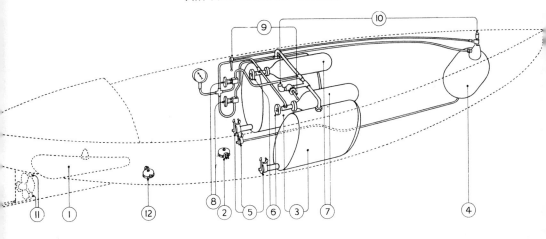

AIR AND BALLAST SYSTEM

1. Hydroplane.	7. Air Bottles.
2. Craft Flooding Valve.	8. Ballast and Trim Tank Blowing Valves.
3. Ballast Tanks.	9. Ballast and Trim Tank Vent Levers.
4. Trim Tank.	10. Ballast and Trim Tank Vents.
5. Kingston Valves.	11. Suction Nozzles for emptying craft.
6. Bottle Isolating Valves.	12. Suction Control Valve.

7. Schematic diagram of the Motor Submersible Canoe known as the *Sleeping Beauty* developed by boat builders Camper and Nicholsons in conjunction with Blondie Hasler.

8. *Sleeping Beauty* under tow.

9. Back row: (left to right) Oxley, Ruff, ?, Fisher, Girving. Second row: Duncan, Turfey, Lambert, Stevens, Colley, Jelks, Harding. Third row: Horner, Major Gordon, Lieutenant Richards, Bill Sparks. Front row: Sergeant King, Corporal Ashton, Sergeant Johnson.

10. Pictured (second from left) with various of my comrades at SAS HQ Haifa. The dog was the SAS mascot.

11. Kit inspection prior to a raid.

12. Launching a Cockle Mark II from a beach.

13. Loading canoes on to Motor Gun-boat.

14. Working with canoes aboard a submarine.

15. An explosive motorboat, never used operationally.

16. Visiting the cellar at Château Magnol, Blanquefort, where Mick Wallace and Jock Ewart were imprisoned.

17. Together with George Ewart, brother of Jock Ewart, in front of the wall where Jock and Mick Wallace were shot. The marks made by the machine-gun fire can still be seen. Also shown is the plaque dedicated to the two heroic marines.

18. My wife Renie and I with veterans of the French Paras at Blanquefort in 1999. François Boisner, who helped establish the *Frankton Walk*, is on the far right.

19. Being presented with a commemorative plaque from the Greek Sacred Squadron by General Kalenderides. In turn I presented the general with a print of Jack Russell's painting 'Cockleshell Heroes'.

20. Seated between two US Marines while on tour in the Baltimore to promote the film *Cockleshell Heroes*.

21. With my dear friend Tony Newley after the opening night of *Scrooge* at the Dominion Theatre. Tony invited Renie and I into his private apartment, but unfortunately it was the last time I saw this lovely man.

22. Representing London Transport on Rememberance Day
at the Cenotaph 1985.

23. Marching proudly beside the Mayor of Portsmouth while on our way to the
unveiling of a plaque dedicated to Operation Frankton in the Rose Gardens at
Southsea in 1989.

24. With Major Conrad Thorpe, RM, outside the château at Blanquefort in December 1999.

25. Admiral Erich Raeder, Commander-in-Chief of the German Navy at the time of Operation Frankton. He was outraged by the execution of our lads and felt the shame deeply.

26. Back on the Rock of Gibraltar for the first time since 1943. I am with Marine Bandmaster Phil Lampton holding a preview of the Royal Naval Philatelic cover issued there on 11 December to commemorate the 50th anniversary of Operation Frankton. I was also publicizing my book *Last of the Cockleshell Heroes*.

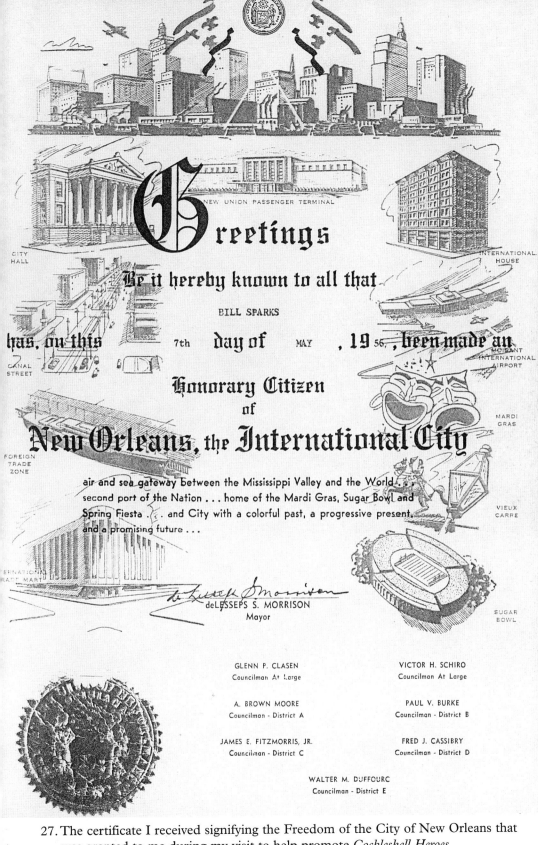

27. The certificate I received signifying the Freedom of the City of New Orleans that was granted to me during my visit to help promote *Cockleshell Heroes*.

28. In training at Canvey Island for another paddle up the Gironde.

29. With the painter, and England cricket star, Jack Russell, and his wonderful painting 'Cockleshell Heroes'. I am so proud to be featured in this work.

30. I had the honour of taking the salute when the Royal Marine Band Beat Retreat at the last Royal Tournament at Earl's Court. It is scandalous that this event has been axed as uneconomic.

31. With the lads of 42 Commando at the last Earl's Court show in November 1999.

32. Paddling up the Thames as part of the ceremony to launch the 1994 Royal British Legion Poppy Appeal. The weather was foul and the fire tender didn't help much either; it gave me a good soaking as I passed by!

beckoned us to follow her upstairs. Soon, we were in a double bed and fast asleep.

A loud knocking at the door brought us up sharp. 'Go and see who it is.' Hasler ordered. 'Why me?' I asked. 'Because I'm a major' he replied with a cheeky grin. To my eternal relief, when I opened the door, instead of the Germans I had half expected, standing in front of me was a little elderly lady. With a smile, and in immaculate English, she said, 'I have brought you some chocolate. Can I come in?' More questions; I got the feeling she was trying to catch us out. Eventually she rose, and left us saying, 'Be ready to leave in one hour. A van will come, and you will be taken to the line of demarcation. Goodbye.' She was genuine. An agent for the French Resistance. It was amazing what risks these wonderful people were prepared to take.

At that time there was a demarcation line running through the middle of France separating the occupied and unoccupied zones. Many French people had escaped to the unoccupied parts, but when the Germans took over the whole of France they set up the demarcation line to prevent those who had escaped, from returning to their original homes. The line was heavily guarded. We would have to cross it.

A knock at the door, and there stood a weasel faced middle aged man, whom I did not like the look of one bit. He led us down to the café and we said our thanks and goodbyes to our hostess. There were no windows in the back of the vehicle – now we were really in the dark! The van stopped about twelve miles from Ruffec, and we climbed out. Much to my delight there was no firing squad waiting for us – just old weasel face! He told us to stay where we were, someone would come and take us across the line. The van left. We stood alone in the dark.

A couple of hours must have elapsed before a figure appeared out of the darkness. Without hesitation this young man in his early teens walked straight up to us, and with an outstretched hand greeted us warmly. He took us near to the edge of a road he said was the line telling us he would cross first and we were to follow one at time on his first and second whistle. Our guide disappeared into the blackness of night. Then came the first whistle. Hasler went off like a rabbit. All was quiet. Then came the second whistle. Leaping through the long grass that led up to the road, I took off like an Olympic sprinter. Seconds later I was across and into some bushes where our guide and the major were waiting. Blondie whispered 'Well done Bill.' We wasted no time. With our guide in the lead, we moved through the wood dodging stealthily in and out of the trees. About half an hour later we came to a farmhouse. Our guide tapped on the door. After introducing us to the young man whose home we were now in, our guide wished us 'bonne chance' and left. (I was reunited with this marvellous man in 1999 and thanked him for all that he did. Sadly, he has since died.)

Our host Monsieur DuBois, made us very welcome and bade his wife to bring us food. After we had eaten we were shown to our room. In it there was a double bed, a couple of chairs, and a table on which several books – in English and French – were laid. Major Hasler asked our congenial host who had organized things for us. He replied that the organization we were now under was led by a woman in the French Resistance known to him as Marie Claire. Blimey, I was thinking with typical cockney chauvinism, 'putting our lives in the hands of a woman'. I was soon to learn that Marie Claire, whose real name was Mary Lindell, Comtesse de Milleville, was both a remarkable and extremely brave woman – to whom I owe my life.

We spent the next few weeks, eating, sleeping, reading newspapers and listening to the radio. Well, Hasler did the reading; I did the listening. During this time I found that he and I had very little in common. I became more impatient than he did.

We spent Christmas 1942 with the DuBois family in their farmhouse. They did their best for us and we could not have been more grateful. But pangs of homesickness began to set in as I thought of my family enjoying a good old London Christmas. Then I considered how much better off I was than those who were POWs and cheered up. To celebrate New Year Madame DuBois cooked us a marvellous meal. Hopefully, it wouldn't be long before we would be back home.

Monsieur DuBois said that at last he had news of Marie Claire, and that her son Maurice would be coming to collect us in a few days. Thus far we had been at the farm for about a month. True to his word, after a few days, Maurice turned up. He was about nineteen years old, good looking and spoke perfect English. To start with, he apologized for the delay in making contact, saying that his mother had been involved in a bad accident in which she was seriously hurt. In fact it wasn't an accident at all, she had been shot by the Germans. Maurice asked, 'Can you ride a bicycle?' When we both replied that we could, he continued, 'First, we will cycle to Roumazières and from there we will catch the train to Lyon.'

We had started to prepare for our journey when Monsieur DuBois came into the room and asked if we had anything on us that was English. I said that all I had was the identity disc that hung around my neck. Monsieur DuBois demanded I hand it over. With some reluctance, I did as he asked. Hasler told him our underwear had English labels on, but said he thought we should keep that on the grounds that it might help to prove we were English – should the need arise. There was an argument but Hasler stood his ground. Now sixty years on, I wonder if DuBois knew something that we did not – but was reluctant to burden us with it?

Wrapping up a parcel that contained a change of underwear Monsieur DuBois passed it to Major Hasler, saying not to let it out of his sight. Hasler passed it to me with the words 'You heard what he said, Bill?' I nodded. We bid our farewells to the DuBois family and collected our bikes. 'But there are only two Maurice.' I observed. 'Yes Bill. I can't ride a cycle. One of you will have to give me a lift on the crossbar.' And so, with our young friend on the crossbar of my bike, we set off.

When we reached the railway station, Maurice told us to stay concealed and wait for his signal to board the train. As yet, we had no false identity cards so Maurice would have to buy the tickets for us. We hid up near some bushes on the far end of the platform. It was not long before a train pulled in. Maurice waited until the last moment before boarding, and as he did so he nodded in our direction. We needed no second bidding; we darted up the platform and boarded the train. I walked through an open carriage and sat on a seat at the far end. I felt someone sit beside me. At first I thought it was Blondie Hasler, but soon realized that it was in fact a German officer! Looking around me, and spotting Maurice and the major, I vacated my seat and joined them. I just hoped that the German didn't think my actions suspicious. Thankfully he remained seated.

When we got to Lyon, Maurice went through the barrier first, followed closely by Hasler. Just as I was about to do likewise a gendarme said something to me that I could not understand, and pointed at the parcel I was carrying. Not understanding a word of what he was saying, I handed the parcel to him and walked on, soon losing myself in amongst the crowd. Outside the station and reunited with my colleagues I explained about the parcel. 'Oh hell,' Hasler blurted out as we hurried away.

We boarded a tram, alighting after a few miles. I don't know why I was alarmed to see so many German soldiers on the streets.

We followed Maurice into a block of flats where he knocked on a door, which was immediately answered. Hasler and I followed him into a small sitting room where he introduced us to a diminutive figure, who was waiting to greet us. 'This is my mother – Marie Claire.' 'I am so sorry you had to stay for so long at the farm. It was because my escape route over the Pyrenees has broken down. As yet I have not opened up a new route. Come, let's have lunch.'

Over lunch Marie Claire kept up a steady stream of questions. She asked where in England I lived. 'The East End of London.' 'I know it well.' Whether she did or not she sounded very convincing. I told her of our hostile encounters with some of the French country folk we had met. She replied that we should have been all right in the region we had passed through. She then asked Major Hasler to say something to her in French and, when he did, she put her arms in the air and said, 'No wonder they were hostile, you speak French with a German accent!' I couldn't help grinning, but the major looked a trifle dismayed at this revelation.

Our stay in Lyon did not pass without incident. We frequently moved addresses. On one such occasion we were travelling by bus when Marie Claire announced in English, in a voice that could be heard by every passenger, that we had reached our destination. I wanted to hide. I was not to know it then, but Hasler kept a secret diary in which he had written, 'The only time I thought of giving myself up while escaping through France, was when I realized I had to shack up with Sparks.' I didn't discover this until 1998 when it was revealed in a book on Blondie Hasler written by Ewen Southby-Tailyour. Had I realized then, that my Commanding Officer felt that way, I might have thought of doing something about it. Marie Claire would certainly have done something about it – had she known.

After what seemed like an eternity, the time came for us to leave the city. With our guides, two RAF escapees, and a Belgian flyer we boarded the train for Perpignan. From there we would cross the Pyrenees. With the identity cards that Marie Claire had arranged for us we passed through the barrier at Perpignan station without fuss. They were as near perfect as one could hope for. Our guides showed us to a table outside a street café, where we waited for about an hour. A van came rumbling along and stopped nearby. Rising as casually as possible we followed our guides to where the van had parked, just out of sight of the café. Soon we were bouncing along, and although I couldn't see a thing, it was obvious that we were climbing.

The van stopped and we got out. We were now at the foot of snow-capped mountains. Our guides climbed back into the van and drove away. We were about to set off on our own when two men appeared. They looked every inch Basques. The two men handed us each a small parcel containing a sweet potato and a pair of canvas shoes. We were told the shoes were essential for the crossing though they didn't look anything like suitable to me. In single file we set off.

The deep snow made for very hard going, and the fact that we were now so unfit didn't help. My lungs were on fire. Eventually we reached the foot of the mountains. After another march we came to a small house where our Basque guides left us. We spent a couple of days with a jovial Spanish host, until our guides returned with a lorry. It was full of toilet seats! We climbed in the back. I was spoilt for choice of places to sit! After a bumpy old ride we arrived in the city and were escorted to an old hotel, where rooms had been prepared for us. The next morning I answered a knock at the door and, to my surprise, standing before me, was a uniformed chauffeur.

With a smart salute, and a smile to match, he said, 'Good morning Sir, I have come to take you to the British Consulate.'

The British consul had arranged for Major Hasler to return to England by plane. Being not nearly as important as Blondie, I was to return to my homeland by ship via Gibraltar. To put the tin lid on it, when I got off the train at Euston station, two Redcaps were waiting for me! I had avoided Germans and gendarmes all these months – only to be arrested by our own military police!

Chapter 2

Return to Southsea

It was early in May 1943 when I stepped off the train at Portsmouth, and slowly made my way toward Southsea, which at that time was still the training area of the SBS. Reaching the promenade and with the barracks in the distance, I stood momentarily, looking across the water towards the end of the South Parade pier. With mixed feelings of fondness and anxiety, I thought of the wonderful comrades with whom I had shared such hazardous times during Operation Frankton. Not, at this time, knowing their fate, I mused, 'Yeah, they would escape all right, just like me and Blondie Hasler did. Every man jack was top class; they would survive.'

It had taken Major Hasler and I almost five months to escape through France, then Spain, and to Gibraltar. During that time we shared many hair-raising experiences, and only evaded capture by the skin of our teeth. Without assistance from the courageous French resistance leader 'Marie Claire' we could not, would not, have made it. We owed her everything.

My mind turned to our last exercise before Frankton. Mick Wallace, our section sergeant, had informed us that there would be no leave that night as he had obtained permission to take us on an exercise. We looked at him aghast, it was Saturday, the night when we went ashore to let our hair down after a hectic week's activities. It was our one respite during the relentless schedule of commando training, and much looked forward to.

Mick himself loved his Saturday night run ashore, so what had come over him? However, he was the boss, and what he said had to be obeyed. It was pointless arguing with Mick. As dusk fell, instead of getting spivved up to take on the town, we grudgingly

26

made our way down to the boathouse. After changing into our canoeing gear, with not a few grumbles we collected our craft. Mick stood by, sporting a huge grin. 'What's he got to bloody smile at', we muttered. With the command of 'Right lads, get water-borne' coming from our sergeant, each crew slide their canoes into the water and climbed aboard.

Once afloat we paddled a short distance out to sea, then turned about and waited for Mick to join and lead us, into whatever he had planned that he was obviously finding so amusing. Still grinning, Mick took up his position in the vanguard of our small flotilla and struck off like a mother swan with her family of cygnets neatly tucked in behind.

During the war, a defensive boom made of scaffolding had been stretched across the water from Southsea to Ryde, on the Isle of Wight. Much to our surprise we penetrated the boom, and headed towards the end of the pier. Previously our exercises had taken us in the opposite direction. It was now quite dark and as we lay off the end of the pier, we could hear, quite plainly, the music coming from the dance band. Saturday night dances were a regular feature on the pier. We stopped paddling and closed up around Mick, who explained, still grinning like a Cheshire cat: at the rear of the dance-hall on the end of the pier, in the area at the back of the stage, the musicians kept their beer in readiness to drink during the brief interval. The object of the exercise was for us to practice our stealth approach. This we were to do by climbing up the stanchions of the pier, unlocking and entering the area behind the stage, then relieving the musicians of their beer.

A hushed chuckle spread amongst the clandestine party. I thought, 'I might have guessed, only Mick could have conjured up this one.' Entering into the spirit of the idea with enthusiasm, we paddled our canoes under the pier. The front man in each canoe grabbed hold of an iron stanchion, allowing his colleague to scale the pier. With extreme caution we approached the door at the back of the dance hall. It opened with surprising ease. Mick's information had been spot on. There before our eyes were crates of bottled beer, waiting for thirsty musicians to sup. We wasted no time in extracting our booty, by stuffing as many bottles as we could carry down the front of our battledress blouses. Soon, we were over the side and back down the stanchions to our mates waiting patiently in the canoes under the cover of the pier. Exercise, or should that be excursion, over, we made our way back to our little hut on the beach, where we consumed our ill-gotten gains. I should have known that Mick wouldn't miss out on a Saturday night booze up!

I was brought swiftly back to reality by the sight of two canoes out at sea and realized that instead of daydreaming I was supposed to be reporting to my new section commander. I wandered along the sea front towards the boathouse, not really relishing joining up with the new section. I passed the barbed wire barrier, which told strangers that this part of the front was out of bounds to all, except us that is. On approaching the boathouse I was greeted with a shout of 'Ned, you old war horse, welcome home.' It had come from Lieutenant Bill Gordon, the section leader himself. With a welcome like this, perhaps my fears were unfounded.

The lads in the section all made a fuss of me, and wanted to hear my story first hand. As much as I would have been happy to accommodate them, at this stage, I was still sworn to secrecy. I did notice quite a few new faces in the unit, and was reminded that this was now number one section, which was not a very happy reminder; it was lads from the former number one section that hadn't returned from the raid on Bordeaux.

I soon became completely engrossed in the work, regardless of the fact that we were now concentrating on underwater swimming more than ever, a part of the training I was never really happy with. Returning to my billet for lunch one day, always eager to see if any mail had arrived for me, I was intrigued to see a very official looking envelope sitting on the end of my bed. I held it for a second, then hastily tore it open to reveal a letter from our supremo, Lord Louis Mountbatten. Typewritten on Combined Operations notepaper and signed personally, it read:

'Dear Sparks, I am delighted to see you have been awarded the Distinguished Service Medal and I am writing to offer you my most sincere congratulations. This is a fitting tribute to the courage and resourcefulness that you showed on your hazardous operation.'

Dumbfounded, I wandered back to the parade not saying a word in case there had been a mistake.

Blondie Hasler, who had been promoted to lieutenant colonel, summoned me and said, 'Congratulations on your award, it was well earned.' There had been no mistake, but I still could not take it in. News travels fast in the corps and everyone congratulated me. But the respect my comrades both old and new showed me, I cherish most. I have never needed much of an excuse for a celebration, and this was no exception. Together with the lads I went out on the town to 'wet' the medal. In such good humour were we, we even managed to avoid a fight with the matelots!

When I walked through the huge gates at Buckingham Palace in a brand new set of blues, it was the proudest moment of my life. My mum and dad had also been invited to the investiture and as we arrived they were escorted along with other guests to the gallery, whilst I was ushered into a room with other recipients. We were briefed in turn about procedure, and how to conduct ourselves. Being the junior I was last in line and on the 'any questions' request, I asked how to address the King should he speak to me. I was told not to worry, His Majesty was much too busy to enter into conversation. A military band was playing as we waited patiently. My name was called. Feeling rather nervous I marched up to the dais as instructed, turned, bowed, and took one step forward. The King placed my treasured medal on the hook I had been told to fix in readiness on the breast of my tunic, then shook my hand and proceeded to ask me all about the raid. At that moment I would have liked a word with the chap who briefed us!

Back at Southsea the colonel had decided that parachuting should be included in our training. Now this really appealed to me – we had done everything else, why not this?

We arrived at the parachute training school at Ringway, Manchester, where we met the instructors. Ours was to be a little cockney, Flight Sergeant Palmer, who had made over 200 jumps. We were in awe of him. With parachute training, fitness is of paramount importance, but this was no hardship for us, we were all quite fit from our own training. Our preparation impressed the sergeant instructor, and we became firm favourites.

First we learned to jump from the shelves with harness on, then from the tower some eighty feet up. It was terrifying at first to be told to launch yourself into space and hoped your harness would hold, but as with most things, the more you do it the more familiar it all becomes.

After the preliminaries, training started in earnest. Our first jump was from the basket of a static balloon, 700 feet up, with our exit to be made via a hole in the floor. The wind was whistling through the rigging and the basket began to sway. Secretly I began to hope that the drop would be cancelled because it was too windy but then I realized that the only real windy thing up here was me! I thought to hell with it and volunteered to go first. Sitting on the edge of the hole, my legs dangling in space, I heard the dreaded orders barked out from my instructor, 'Action stations number one – go.' I launched my body through the hole, not knowing what to expect. The wind was now whistling past my ears, I glanced up at my canopy, and could see that it hadn't yet opened. Panic set in, and I began thinking 'my God, my first jump and I've bought it' when I suddenly stopped falling and began floating majestically. Looking upwards I could see my canopy was fully open – a beautiful sight.

I felt ten feet tall and now wanted the jump to go on forever. Glancing down, however, I saw that the ground was getting ever nearer and in fact was now rushing to meet me! My mind ran through the landing drill, but I need not have worried. Had I forgotten anything a sharp reminder was on hand in the form of an instructor on the ground bellowing advice through a loud hailer – they didn't leave much to chance at Ringway. I met mother earth with a copybook landing.

The old Whitley bomber trundled across the airfield, and gradually gathered speed, until she gently lifted off. This was our first jump from a plane. There were ten of us in the stick and I was to be first man out. As the aircraft approached the dropping zone our instructor lifted the cover revealing the ubiquitous hole in the floor through which we would drop. I took up position, my legs dangling into space, and waited for a signal from the dispatcher. My eyes were glued to the red light above me, whilst I waited anxiously. Then the green light illuminated, and was quickly followed by a slap on the back and a bellow in my ear – 'Go.' I dropped into space like a stone. Unlike the balloon jump when I worried about the time it was taking for my canopy to open, the movement of the plane pulled the static line away and forced the chute open almost before I could think about it, and I floated gently down to earth.

We made a further five daylight drops from the old aircraft

without incident. Then came a drop in the dark from the balloon, once more at 700 feet, and as before I was first out. It was a splendid moonlit night and floating gently down was a wonderful feeling. Somehow it seemed to be taking longer than I had remembered. I could see the earth coming to meet me and waited until I thought I was about 10 feet from the ground before giving my quick release box a bang. Shrugging off the harness that held me, I stepped onto mother earth; only there was none! My night vision had deceived me and I simply kept falling. I misjudged the distance by at least 20 feet, finally landing with such force that it sent shock waves throughout my body. I rolled over onto my back thinking I must have caused myself serious injury. Fortunately I had broken nothing and was just badly winded. Having recovered, I ran off to join the rest of the group who were still waiting to go up. 'Nothing to it,' I lied.

The course for the army parachutists had concluded. There was to be a parade the next day where all those who had passed the rigorous tests would be presented with their wings. We marines were not included; there would be no presentation of wings for us. As special forces we were classified secret, and were still operating under the guise of being a group of marines routinely patrolling the boom at Southsea.

A request came from our commanding officer that before returning to our base we should do a drop into water. The lumbering Whitley took us over a large lake where this time I was waiting halfway down the stick. We had been told to treat the jump the same as for a ground landing, except we must release our chutes at about 15 feet. If we still had them on when entering the water, there was a real danger of the canopy enveloping the parachutist and drowning him. I thought thank goodness it's daylight, my night-time judgement of distance would cause a mighty splash. The drop went without mishap and we returned to Southsea.

Back at base we were informed that our colonel had been sent to the Far East to take charge of a unit of the Special Boat Squadron (SBS) out there, and that we were to follow him in the near future. This was fine for the rest of the lads, but not for me. I had been detailed to stay behind to help train another section. This went against the grain, so I went to the office to protest.

Thanks to my parachute instructor's recommendation I had been promoted to the rank of corporal, this of course weakened my argument to accompany the unit to the Far East. Furthermore I was told that since I had only recently been in enemy territory, I could not be drafted for at least six months. My only way out was to volunteer, so despite what my old dad had always said, 'Never volunteer for anything', I did. Should a non commissioned officer (NCO) drop out for any reason whatsoever, I would be first reserve.

Time was getting very close to embarkation, but with no sign of any NCOs dropping out. Then my old friend Bill Ellery (who had been with me on Frankton, although he never took part in the raid itself due to his canoe being damaged prior to launching) now a corporal himself, confided in me that he had a domestic problem that needed urgent attention. He couldn't get leave at this late stage, so in desperation had decided to go absent without leave (AWOL). This would obviously eliminate him from the draft and I would have to take his place. He apologized profusely – I was overjoyed!

The weekend passed without event. On the Monday morning the section fell in on the parade ground and the roll was called. Ellery's name was called out with no response. So my pal had done what he had said he would do – gone AWOL. Questions were asked but in the time-honoured 'I know nothing about it Sir' tradition, no one offered any explanation as to what had happened to the missing corporal. It was the section commander's duty to inform the reserve, who of course was me, that I would have to take the place of the missing man. He approached with a wry smile saying, 'You're happy now, are you?' Excitement was at fever pitch and we were ordered to prepare our stores and kit for transit to Scotland, where we would undergo further training.

We arrived at the small town of St Andrews, made famous by its championship golf course, a place of beauty. But what of the locals, how would they react to our presence there? Stories abounded on the dour Scottish humour.

We were allocated our billets, and what luck when I found that along with three others I was to stay in the Bluebell Hotel, a delightful little pub. Our host and hostess were two of the most generous and friendly souls you will ever meet. Jessie, our landlady, was like a mother to us, even to the extent of putting hot water bottles in our beds at night! Dave, Jessie's husband, sometimes invited me down to the cellar at closing time, fobbing his wife off with the excuse that he wanted to teach me how to tap barrels.

Once in the cellar out would come Dave's special malt whisky, kept only for such occasions, and we would sit down with the bottle and discuss how best to win the war.

All good things come to an end, and this was to be no exception. Our stay in Scotland was over all too soon. With tearful farewells from our host and his caring wife, we entrained for Liverpool where a ship was docked in readiness to take us to the Far East.

Chapter 3

Embark for the Aegean Sea

The first morning aboard ship we awoke to find we were still in Liverpool docks, delayed until there were sufficient vessels to form a convoy. Enemy U-boats were very active during this period of the war. Slowly the convoy began to build, but it was a further three days before enough ships were gathered and we were able to get underway.

Flanked by our escort of Hunt class destroyers we entered the Irish Sea. Typical of that particular stretch of water, there was a heavy swell going, and our troopship began to pitch then roll causing the lesser sailors among us to lose their supper. My previous sea service stood me in good stead so I kept mine down.

The days passed boringly, with the only excitement coming from the activity of the destroyers when, having picked up a contact on their Asdic these little hunters circled and crossed with an amazing turn of speed in an effort to locate the enemy submarine. We thrilled to see the destroyers firing off their depth charges, then hoped for a 'kill', with the bow of a sub appearing. I gave a thought to the fate of the submariners entombed in the metal casing with all engines shut down, sitting on the sea bed hoping the enemy would pass them by. This was a dog eat dog war and if I had to fight it from the sea, I think I would prefer to have been on a destroyer – certainly not in a submarine

A few days later, in the middle of the night, we could see in the distance, the lights of Spain. My thoughts turned to my escape through the Pyrenees after the raid on Bordeaux. Although Spain was supposed to be neutral, they would have interned me in awful conditions had I been caught. Under cover of darkness we slipped through the Straits of Gibraltar. Looming above us was my old friend the Rock. I saluted her as we passed. I recalled the events in early 1941 when I was serving aboard the battle cruiser *Renown,* as she came about to take up her place in the convoy, which was heading for the beleaguered Island of Malta. With *Renown* adding considerable weight to our escort of destroyers, two light cruisers and an aircraft carrier, we were pretty well defended. At that time, with the battle raging in the desert the whole theatre of war was pretty volatile. Adding to the threat of enemy action was El Duce [Mussolini] himself, who had made a promise to his partner-in-crime Adolf Hitler, that no British ship would enter the Mediterranean, as that sea belonged to him. We were about to show the Italian dictator just how wrong he was.

Two uneventful days passed; nevertheless gun crews were continually closed up around their weapons in readiness for any surprises the enemy might have in store. Then, faintly at first, we heard the distinctive drone of aircraft – getting louder by the minute. The air raid alarm was sounded and everyone 'stood to' as the enemy planes approached at very high altitude.

Every gun in our small fleet barked in defiance: 20 × 4.5-inch guns blasted away from *Renown*. Almost at once two enemy planes fell from the sky, crashing in flames into the sea. Our defensive barrage was so intense it kept the enemy aircraft at a height that made it difficult for them to hit their intended targets.

The battle raged for some hours as wave after wave of aircraft were beaten off. Eventually the enemy planes turned tail without having sunk a single ship. The Italian pilots were not particularly renowned for low flying under fire. Instead they stayed high out of range, but they couldn't hit much from up there! In fact they didn't much like close encounters of any kind – except in peacetime that is (lock up your daughters)! Italian servicemen in the majority never really had their heart in their leader's cause. When calm was restored we were allowed to relax a little, although we remained closed up around our guns.

The following day dawned in brilliant sunshine, with the reflections from the sea making it difficult, without squinting, to see the horizon. It was hard to believe there was a war on. Alarm bells going off once again soon shattered our peaceful cruise. Our guns were trained skywards in readiness for an air attack but we were in for a surprise. Instead of planes at high altitude, the first sortie made its attack wave top high. Winding our guns back to a level position we realized that the enemy had changed tactics. The Italian flyers had been exchanged for the Luftwaffe, a different kettle of fish altogether. They hit us relentlessly, whilst they in turn were much harder for us to hit at that height. Soon there were ships on fire and sinking. Our gallant little destroyers rushed about picking up survivors, whilst at the same time keeping their ears tuned to their Asdic sets. The threat from enemy submarines was ever present, and we didn't need any torpedoes fired at us right now.

The sun went down and the battle ceased. Thankfully, when it peeked its shimmering head over the horizon the next day we were close enough to Malta to hand over the remains of our convoy to the Eastern Mediterranean Fleet.

With the desert war over and our troops now fighting in Italy, the threat to us from the air had diminished. However the U-boats were still out there somewhere, stalking their prey. It was a comfort to have our destroyers patrolling, thus keeping the enemy at bay. The port of Alexandria loomed ahead as we made our dawn approach. Eagerly we waited as the coastline became clearer, and familiar to those of us who had happy memories of 'good old days' when we were stationed there. What fortune now awaited us, good or bad, we knew not.

Our trooper entered the harbour and made its way straight to the dockside. This was an unusual practice for a passing convoy, as visiting ships would normally anchor in the middle of the harbour. Curiosity got the better of us and as we watched stores being unloaded, 'bingo', we recognized some of our own gear. Perhaps we were to get a run ashore after all.

Our CO gathered us about him, informed us that we were stopping off here, and told us to collect our kit immediately. Intrigued, we dashed below, grabbed our kitbags and re-assembled on the quayside. As a 3-ton truck took us to an army camp nearby we chatted among ourselves, 'Why are we disembarking here, when we were bound for the Far East?' We didn't have to wait long for an explanation, for our CO called us together once more and said, 'The reason we are disembarking in Alex, is because the crew on one of our friendly merchant ships has mutinied. Now they are threatening to leave our convoy and take their ship back to their native land. Our job will be to put their vessel out of action thus preventing them from sailing.' Word of our expertise in this particular field had travelled fast, although the prospect of disabling a 'friendly' merchantman was not a job that any of us particularly relished.

That same evening, as dusk fell, we prepared our limpet mines for the job in hand. The task was merely to prevent them from moving the ship, not to sink it – easier said than done. As we were about to enter the water our CO came scuttling among us telling us to hold fast, and that the attack had been called off – it transpired that the mutinous seamen had relented and agreed to obey their captain. It must have been a bluff, but if it was, we weren't aware of it. Surely we wouldn't have been allowed to put a hole in a perfectly seaworthy vessel?

By this time, under the cover of darkness, the rest of our convoy had left for the Far East; we wondered what would befall us now. The prospect of a run ashore in the famous port was one thing, but none of us fancied anything more permanent. Our major gave us a few hours off to go ashore for a pint, at the same time informing us that we would receive further instructions the next morning. In the armed services it is generally accepted that the rank and file is more or less kept in the dark until the last minute, so you can imagine the conversation that took place over a drink and the diverse ideas put forward as to our immediate future.

Next morning we awoke full of expectation, and were not disappointed to learn that we were leaving the same day to join up with the Special Air Service in Haifa. The SAS boys were busy raiding enemy-held Greek Islands, but the Germans had two destroyers in the Aegean that were causing some concern, so it would be up to us to put them out of action. 'Now this is more like it,' we chorused, 'right up our street.' It was with excitement, and the expectation of the action to come, that we waited for transport to take us to the railway station in Alexandria.

The usual 3-tonner arrived and we bundled our kit and stores onto it. Unaware of the harassment we were to encounter on our journey, it was with a light heart that we pulled out of the station in Alex. A journey that should have taken no more than a few hours lasted three days! Eventually, sweaty and fed up, we arrived in Haifa and were picked up by the customary 3-tonner and transported to the SAS camp on the outskirts of the town.

The camp was, quite understandably, in a desolate part of the country, yet we warmed to it instantly. An air of camaraderie exuded from the inhabitants and was immediately extended to us.

These boys were a happy-go-lucky bunch who had already seen plenty of action in the desert campaign. We were welcomed by the camp adjutant and shown to our quarters. We were somewhat surprised to be allocated wooden chalets, considering the 'Regiment' was under canvas. We had no complaints, our accommodation was comfortable indeed given the conditions of the day, and we settled in soon enough.

We didn't have long to wait before orders came through detailing six men with three canoes to proceed to the Aegean Sea. To my dismay, I was not in the party selected. The reason given, was that, as I had already done a raid, they would use this opportunity to blood those who hadn't. A truck loaded with men and canoes sped off into the night, and those of us left behind wished them God-speed. Whilst we were all keen to see some action, we were, quite naturally, a little apprehensive. This was new territory for us, and we didn't have much idea of the conditions we would operate under. However, we were all quite confident that our comrades would give a good account of themselves.

Chapter 4

Leros

With the raiding party of six marines on board, the truck arrived at the docks in Beirut. The men quickly transferred their stores to a three-masted caique tied up alongside the harbour wall. With marines and their gear on board, the sailing vessel slid quietly out of the harbour and headed towards the Aegean. There would be many hazards to pass en route, but although this method of sea transport was slow it was also practically silent, which was of the utmost importance given the nature of the task embarked upon.

Dawn crept over the horizon and in glorious sunlight the schooner cleft its passage through the shimmering blue Mediterranean Sea. It was so peaceful. With the daylight gradually fading and the island of Crete just about visible, the schooner veered away from its coastline and welcomed darkness when it fell. To avoid this island was vital. Crete was heavily defended, and patrolled by German E-boats that could quite easily outrun anything the British Navy had in the Aegean.

The plan was to keep as close as possible to the Turkish coast and head for the uninhabited island of Kastelorizon, an island long evacuated by the enemy and left in ruins after numerous attacks from the air. Although considered of little use by our adversaries, it made a fairly safe haven for our raiding forces.

The caique glided into the small harbour entrance, and our vigilant lookouts kept watch for any unexpected activity on the island, or unwanted vessels in the vicinity. The boat moored alongside the jetty, and as swiftly as was practicable unloaded its cargo of marines and their gear. Whilst the marines took cover, the caique turned about and left as silently as it had arrived.

The raiding party made themselves as comfortable as they could in a bombed out villa, and waited for their next transport, a small gunboat, to arrive. At dawn, a vessel was spotted approaching the island, and the marines stood to. In silence, and with not some level of apprehension, the raiders concentrated of the shape of the vessel until it was sufficiently close enough to be identified as one of ours.

Cautiously the little gunboat nosed its way into the harbour entrance, with the young sailors on board manning the armament, which consisted of a Bofors gun on the forecastle, and a pair of twin Vickers machine guns amidships, to port and starboard. These little gunboats were the largest we had in the Aegean at the time and, whilst these boats were no match for the enemy's E-boats, the spirited crews of these small fighting vessels were always eager to put to sea.

The marine raiding party ran joyfully down to the harbour to welcome their transport, and after exchanging a brief greeting, set about the task of loading their canoes and equipment on board. As soon as this was completed the gunboat made to leave. There was always a feeling of anxiety from both marines and crew when entering or leaving the harbours of the small unoccupied islands. You felt a bit like a fly escaping from a spider's web – extremely lucky to be free, and underway once more.

As the gunboat approached the island of Leros, the weather conditions could not have been more perfect if they had been ordered. Without an appearance from the moon, the still inky blackness made it ideal for raiding. The sea was calm, with just a hint of swell as the gunboat hove to.

The raiding party was to be led by a young Welsh lieutenant named Jasper Richards, ably supported by his number two, another popular young Welshman by the name of Taffy Stevens. Also in the party were Johnny Horner and Eric Fisher.

(Eric had also been with me on Operation Frankton but took no part in the raid. He would have been in the canoe with Bill Ellery, had it not been damaged whilst launching.) The matelots lowered the first canoe into the water and the officer and his number two climbed down. Once settled in the canoe they were handed their weapons and limpet mines. Two more canoes followed the same procedure. Then the three small boats, with their occupants and deadly cargo, pushed away from the gunboat.

The plan was quite simple, in theory that is. The canoes would enter the harbour, identify the targets, attack with limpet mines, then withdraw, paddling swiftly back to the gunboat, which would be waiting at the location where they had been dropped.

The canoes paddled silently in line towards the entrance to the harbour. Once inside, the ships they intended to attack were instantly recognizable. Jasper signalled to the other canoes, to raft up alongside him. His men now close, in a whisper, he allocated the targets to be attacked by each canoe. Slowly, the first canoe approached a large vessel. Adhering to the strict drill they had practised so many times, they lay very low in the canoe, to minimize the silhouette, and used single paddles to proceed with as little bodily movement as possible. The stern of the enemy ship loomed above as them as they closed up to it. Taffy placed his magnetic holdfast against the side of the ship, to prevent the canoe from drifting with the tide. Richards lowered the rod on which a limpet was attached and clamped the magnetic mine to the ship's hull, below the waterline. Taffy released his magnetic holder, allowing the canoe to drift along the side of the enemy destroyer until they reached mid-ships, when Taffy once again clamped on, whilst Richards placed another limpet mine on the vessel, again below the waterline. So far so good. Taffy removed his magnetic clamp and the canoe drifted towards the bow of their victim. There the demolition procedure was repeated. Still no alarm had sounded. With a level of contentment at having completed their task, the first canoe started to withdraw to the sanctuary of the waiting gunboat.

The second canoe approached its target with as much ease as the first, and following procedure to the letter the crew successfully placed their limpet mines on the target they had been allocated. They, too, could now make their withdrawal.

The third canoe, named *Shrimp*, with Johnny Horner and Eric Fisher in, did not do nearly as well as their counterparts, mainly through faults of their own making. Observing the success of their colleagues and brimming with confidence, they abandoned all they had been taught about paddling in low profile and set off in an upright position. Using double paddles they approached their target at great speed. Needless to say they didn't get far before they were spotted and challenged by a sentry on board the vessel they had targeted. Our training had advised that if challenged we were to 'freeze' and let the canoe drift, when hopefully we would be mistaken for flotsam – there was always plenty of this around in harbours, and even more in wartime.

Challenged for a second time, the likely lads, deciding on tactics of their own invention, answered their challenger with, 'Brandenburger Patroller', though how they expected the Cockney accent of Johnny Horner to pass for German is beyond me. The sentry, now convinced he had the enemy in his sight, offered a further and more aggressive challenge. Realizing it would be futile to continue, the lads in the canoe declared their intention to come alongside and surrender. This was a very dangerous decision indeed and not only for them – under Hitler's Commando Order, issued in 1942, captured commandos were to be shot, after interrogation with no methods barred. Their action could also have jeopardized the whole operation, and also the lives of their comrades. I would have thought that at least Fisher should have known better, being the more experienced of the two.

The two marines paddled their canoe alongside the ship they had targeted, looking for a way to climb aboard her. Finding no ladder or rope to shin up, they decided to paddle around the other side of the vessel to see what was there. Still they found no means of getting aboard the ship. Realizing they were no longer being observed, they paddled under the flare of the bow, along the side of the ship, and then quietly made toward the harbour entrance. Miraculously, they got away from the island, and rendezvoused with the other canoes and the gunboat.

Soon the little gunboat was steaming back to Kastelorizon, where it deposited the marines and their equipment. All the raiding party had to do now was hole up and wait for the caique to come and take them off the island, and return them to base camp.

Meanwhile, we, who had been left behind, anxiously waited for the return of our comrades, eager to know of their exploits. It was with a sense of relief and ecstasy that we greeted them when the raiding party eventually arrived. Congratulations were offered for a successful operation, and gratitude that every man had returned unharmed. We sat around and chatted into the early hours, savouring every morsel of the action.

Some weeks later we heard through our intelligence bods that the two destroyers the lads had attacked were still out of action, and unlikely to make an appearance in the near future.

Chapter 5

Malta and the Aegean

Life in the camp had begun to adopt that dreary monotonous feeling, when out of the blue the ubiquitous 3-tonner pulled up outside our chalets. I thought, 'Here we go, another job in the offing. I only hope that this time it includes me.' I had little time to dwell on the prospect before our CO called us together and explained that a small party was needed for a little 'job' in Malta. My spirits were lifted when the Major called my name as one of a party of six marines who were to accompany him on the 'do'.

We were driven to an airstrip on the outskirts of Haifa where an old Dakota aeroplane waited for us on the runway. We boarded the plane with the minimum of fuss and were soon underway. The old kite taxied for a while then turned into the wind. The pilot opened the throttles and the plane rumbled down the runway and soon we were airborne leaving Palestine behind us and heading for our destination.

When we landed in Malta a reception party was waiting to collect and transfer us to the submarine base. This was the first inkling we had that the job in hand involved a sub. I was not over-joyed at the prospect. As the only member of the party who had experienced a passage in a submarine, I was the only one worried about it!

Together with our equipment we boarded the U-class sub. This type of submarine was one of the smallest in the British Navy, so with six more men added to the crew, and three canoes plus stores and explosives, the accommodation was cramped to say the least. Soon we were making some headway and I could not avoid a feeling of déjà vu reminiscent of the Frankton raid when HMS *Tuna* conveyed us to the mouth of the Gironde River. The officer

43

briefed us on the task that lay ahead. We were on our way to the island of Crete, where we would launch our canoes, paddle them stealthily into the harbour, then attack, with the use of limpet mines, the shipping moored within its confines.

Frankly, I thought this a bit of a tall order because it had long been established that Crete was very heavily defended, with added emphasis placed on its harbour defences. The journey was slow and uneventful and boredom was setting in, when the skipper announced that we were now at periscope depth and approaching our destination. We waited for darkness and as it fell we surfaced. No one was more surprised and shocked than the captain of the submarine when to his, and our dismay, we realized we had surfaced slap-bang in the middle of an incoming enemy convoy. We were now completely surrounded by their escort vessels! Obviously we couldn't even contemplate disembarking, so our quick thinking skipper decided to join the convoy and hope their escorts would be far too busy looking for enemy subs lurking on the edge of the fleet to notice us. Our ploy worked for a time and we cruised un-hindered, that is until a sharp-eyed lookout spotted us and signalled his vessel to close on us for recognition. Our luck had run out. The game was up. Soon the air was filled with machine-gun fire, with bullets raking the side of our sub and ricocheting off the metal casing. Luckily the weapons employed against us were not of sufficient calibre to do any real damage and we crash dived. I did not like this one bit. Soon we were settled on the sea bed and waiting for the inevitable. We didn't have long to wait before we could hear the thud, thud of engines, as our attacker passed overhead. Then silence, followed by a mighty bang as a depth charge exploded. The small sub rocked and rolled as the shock wave caught her, and we were deafened by the noise reverberating around the sub's hull. Then, once more, all was quiet.

We took stock, but nothing seemed to be damaged and everyone was okay. Then, just as we thought that maybe we had got away with it, there came an almighty thump that shook us around like salt in a packet of Smith's crisps. Thankfully we had not suffered a direct hit, although it must have been pretty bloody close. We could hear the now familiar sound of vessels above us. Only this time there was the additional sound of Asdic charges pinging against the hull of the sub; it confirmed our worst fears – the enemy knew exactly where we were.

Thankfully our skipper was experienced and a past master when it came to cat and mouse evasion tactics. He used all his skill to put the enemy off the track, and although we did get a bit of a buffeting from yet another depth charge, gradually we slipped out of their web. Our avoiding action had lasted nearly four hours when finally, under the cover of darkness, the skipper brought the little sub to the surface. We were now well away from the island and breathed a sigh of relief. I could not help thinking; 'This has done sod all to improve my fondness for submarine travel!'

Dawn broke and as per drill instruction we went to our diving stations. The sub slid under the waves and levelled out at periscope depth while the skipper scanned the horizon. He spotted a small caique and sounded a buzzer to alert the crew, and at the same time ordered 'slow ahead' as we closed on it. With the benefit of a closer look at the vessel and deciding it did not impose any kind of threat, the captain gave the order to surface.

Approaching the caique we observed someone waving to us and as we drew alongside our CO prepared to board. It transpired the only crew aboard was one old Greek, who had left his island and wanted to join us. The old man had brought with him his entire wealth, millions of drachmas, crammed into a small attaché case. Now he insisted the money be distributed among us as a reward for his liberation. Sadly, the currency was worthless, but we did have a bit of a laugh waving it about pretending to be millionaires; it did ease the tension somewhat.

A short while before we had been under threat of destruction, and now we were all laughing our socks off – the fortunes of war.

Our CO said we could not leave the caique to drift aimlessly, so decided to employ some of our explosives to sink it. The major had just finished the task of laying the explosives, when as from nowhere an aircraft appeared. The officer scrambled back on board the sub and the skipper prepared to crash dive, but not before the plane had spotted us. Then came the now familiar rat-a-tat as bullets from the plane's machine guns spattered the steel hull of the sub. Fortunately for us the enemy aircraft was not fitted with anything heavy enough to penetrate the casing of our boat, but we knew that he would send a radio message for someone to come out after us.

All next day we remained submerged and only occasionally rose to periscope depth to take a 'butcher's'. It seemed the enemy had given up on us, and we continued to cruise unhindered. Signals were sent from our sub to Malta informing the high command of the reasons why the raid had been aborted. We waited anxiously for instructions, and were well pleased when the order came through ordering us back to Malta.

The dark submarine slid quietly back into Malta's harbour, and after some sweet manoeuvring, tied up alongside the quay of the submarine base. The boat's crew and we marines disembarked and settled into the naval barracks, where for the next few days we happily stayed until our shore legs returned. Able to walk without a wobble once more, we proceeded to a rest camp. This we were told was normal routine for submariners after a long patrol. It was a chance to relieve some of the tension we had built up during our aborted raid. The build up of adrenaline was still present in our systems. The feeling, although great, takes time to recede, during which it is difficult to relax.

Our rest period at an end, we boarded the old Dakota once more and took off for Egypt. Airborne again, Malta became just a memory. A few hours later saw us circling the pyramids, the famous landmarks becoming ever clearer as we made our descent. The ground rushed up to meet us, then with a bump we touched terra firma and the pilot brought the great lumbering aircraft to a standstill.

As expected, waiting for us and our gear on the airstrip was our friendly 3-tonner. With not quite the enthusiasm we showed when we started out on our escapade, we loaded our canoes and equipment onto the lorry, climbed aboard and settled as best we could in preparation for a long trip. Soon we were bumping along on our way back to Haifa.

About halfway across the Sinai Desert, the 3-tonner began to think it had had enough of this tedious journey and, with a fit of coughing and spluttering, gave up the ghost. We ground to a standstill. Although we did have sufficient food and water in case of just such an emergency, it didn't solve the problem of how we were going to repair the motor. The nearest repair facility was a Royal Electrical Mechanical Engineers (REME) workshop, about fifty miles away.

As dusk fell we prepared ourselves for a night in the desert under the stars. We seemed surrounded by miles and miles of sand, without a hint of life in any direction, when, suddenly, a movement ahead caught my eye. I blinked, did a double-take, and no, I wasn't imagining it. Up ahead, sitting in the middle of the dusty road was an Arab. Just where he came from we would never know. We didn't have long to ponder on our situation before we were aware that the fellow up the road was not alone. One by one, more Arabs appeared. They kept their distance and, sitting around in little groups, watched our every movement. We had been warned that such an incident was likely. The ploy of the Arabs was to wait until they were sure we were asleep then move in on us and pluck us like chickens, stealing everything they could lay their thieving hands on.

Bit by bit the circle of vultures closed in, preparing for the kill. When they got what we thought was too close for comfort, to show we meant business we fired a volley over their heads. This stopped them in the tracks and they retreated a distance, but they hadn't given up by any means, which meant we had to keep watch all night. We stationed ourselves around the 3-ton truck, keeping in close contact, and bleary-eyed we waited for dawn. When it came, the Arabs had vanished just as mysteriously as they had appeared. Thankfully they left empty-handed.

We made a fire to get a brew going, the staple diet of the English, tea, what else! We chatted about the events of the previous night and how it could have got out of hand. We were still feeling a bit jittery when the silence was broken by the sound of an engine. Sure enough in the distance we could see a small truck making its way towards us. All we could do now was wait and hope that it was friend and not foe that we were about to encounter.

Thankfully the truck was a British Army one, and the driver pulled up alongside our stricken vehicle. We gave our saviours a cup of tea, and they promised to report our position to the REME workshops. As the small truck disappeared over the horizon, quiet and emptiness surrounded us. The thought of being stranded in the middle of the desert didn't bear thinking of. Eventually your bones would get picked; after the Arabs had had your gear of course!

It seemed like a lifetime, but in fact it was only a few hours later that we heard the sound of a heavy vehicle coming our way. You can imagine our delight to see a REME recovery vehicle advancing toward us. The engineers greeted us with good-natured banter as they leapt down. It didn't take the REME lads long to effect the necessary repairs to our lorry and in no time we were on our way. We said our goodbyes to our rescuers, and one of them replied with: 'We don't expect to have to rescue the bloody Navy in the desert!' This brought a round of laughter from everyone. In wartime, it didn't matter which branch of the services you were in, you were all 'in it' together and had no intention of letting each other down.

As we turned off the road and swung through the entrance to the camp, a gallant little sentry, who challenged us and asked for a password, blocked our path. Because we had been away for so long we had no idea of what the current password was. It was changed regularly for obvious reasons. The major jumped from the vehicle and approaching the sentry, explained to the soldier why he did not know the password, saying he would be most grateful if the sentry would inform him of it. The luckless soldier, obviously not infantry, (they were much sharper that those from the various corps attached who thought it a cheek to be asked to perform duties of this nature) pleased at being asked by a major for his advice puffed out his chest and gave the word. We drove through the barrier with hoots of laughter emanating from the rear of the truck. I think the sentry got his marching orders (excuse the pun). Haifa suddenly looked glamorous – we felt grateful and lucky to be home.

A trifle weary, we settled into the camp routine in anticipation of not having to wait too long to be set some task or other, before the inevitable boredom began to set in. Our prayers were answered by an instruction that our entire ten-man unit was to move. Enter the ubiquitous 3-tonner. Loaded with canoes, equipment and marines our vehicle pulled out of the base. As the camp disappeared in a haze of heat and dust we wondered when, or indeed if, we would ever see it again.

A few hours later saw us pulling up alongside the jetty in Beirut. I for one got an immense feeling of relief when I saw, tied alongside and waiting for us, the old faithful three-masted caique, and not, thankfully, a submarine. The coming journey would be slow and exposed, but I much prefer the fresh air to the claustrophobic atmosphere of a sub.

Knowing that the coming voyage would take several days, it was important to make ourselves as comfortable as possible. There were no sleeping quarters as such, we just bedded down where we could on the upper deck. The first two days were uneventful and mostly very pleasant, however the third one saw us approaching the danger zone. Darkness fell as we entered hostile waters.

Hugging the Turkish coastline, our immediate worry was sailing passed the island of Rhodes without detection. This island was heavily defended, and to make matters worse a powerful searchlight swept the sea in search of intruders such as we. As we peered through the darkness, gradually the silhouette of the island came into view; we were even afraid to talk among ourselves for fear of our voices travelling across the water.

Rhodes seemed menacingly close and we prayed that their listeners were off duty. With bated breath we watched the black shape of the island loom up as though towering over us, whilst the searchlight swept across the water missing us by the narrowest of margins. Hastily our skipper hoisted the Turkish flag hoping this might fool the enemy if the light caught us. We were so close to the island that the big guns installed there would have had no trouble blowing us out of the water, or alternatively they could have sent a dreaded E-boat after us. Either way our fate would have been settled.

Painfully slowly, the old caique rolled and creaked as it slid past the ominous great mass of rock that dominated the vicinity. Gradually, and to my great joy, we left Rhodes behind; we had passed undetected. Now we must make for some kind of shelter, before daylight exposed us to anyone who happened to be around. Thankfully, our skipper was an old hand at avoidance, and as dawn approached he steered his vessel into a beautiful little bay; it was obvious he had done this before.

We dropped anchor in Turkish waters, and later with the sun high and shining gloriously, I decided that if this was a taste of 'the blue' I was going to enjoy it. Much later on I was to find out otherwise. We enjoyed our playboy lifestyle for three days. We were swimming and lying about in the sunshine, when the tranquillity was interrupted by the throb of a powerful motor boat engine. Convinced it was an E-boat, every man armed himself. In a few seconds we were bristling with Brens and Stens cocked ready for action, plus a few grenades to lob to welcome the visitors. Let them come. We would give them a bloody warm reception.

The engines of the powerful craft throttled back, and the bow wave calmed as the craft entered the bay. We thought the vessel was an MTB (motor torpedo boat) but not one that any of us could identify. We dropped to the deck of the sailing boat and with itchy fingers on the triggers of our weapons, waited for our officer to give the command to open fire. We were waiting for the crew of the unidentified boat to show themselves, before sweeping the deck of their craft with fire – before they had a chance to gain the upper hand.

Our CO, Major Bill Gordon, lay on the deck beside us armed only with a pistol. Although he was not expected to take part in any operations, he was a fine officer and was determined to be in the thick of it. This would be his baptism of fire, and we wondered how he would react. As the mysterious boat entered the lagoon it presented a sitting target. Much to our surprise there seemed to be only one person on the craft and he was not wearing a uniform. Suddenly, the captain of our caique came running along the shore, shouting 'friend – friend'! We eased our trigger fingers and waited for our Greek skipper to offer an explanation. Fortunately he spoke pretty good English, and told us that the boat we were about to blow out of the water, was in fact the transport to take us onward to our destination.

The powerful vessel that we now eagerly viewed was a captured Italian torpedo boat. Because it was so noisy it was thought unsuitable for normal operations and so had been stripped of its torpedo tubes to make it lighter, and therefore faster. In fact it could outrun anything the Germans had in the Aegean. This of course boosted morale among us marines considerably; it was the perfect vessel for raiding forces. I quite fancied a bit of a chase.

The Italian boat was named *Naz*; as soon as we got our hands on it we wasted little time in transferring all of our stores and weapons to it. The transfer completed, the skipper of the *Naz* was eager to get underway and take us to our collecting point, Kastelerizon. There we would hole up and wait for a naval gunboat to take us onward.

The Italian boat fairly flew over the waves; it was exhilarating. In no time at all we reached Kastelerizon and all too soon made ready to part company with the *Naz*, as our island of refuge bade us welcome. We disembarked and the skipper of the powerful boat wasted no time in turning about and making his exit. As soon as the boat was clear of the tiny harbour its captain opened the throttles and with a mighty roar the vessel quickly disappeared from view. We gathered up our kit and weapons, and made our way among the ruins trying to find the least damaged building to lay up in. We also had to make sure that we did not put ourselves in a position where the enemy could take us by surprise. They were known to patrol these unoccupied islands at random.

We spent three glorious days exploring our surroundings, delighting in the fig trees and grape vines that were in abundance. We made many fruitless attempts to catch octopus, but although they were plentiful in the bay, they managed to elude us.

If you can catch one, once dried by the sun the tentacles are good to eat. Using any kind of artificial light was quite out of the question, or we could be spotted from miles away, so reluctantly when dusk fell we had to bed down too.

The fourth day, we heard the familiar throb of a motor boat once again. Quickly, we moved into our defence positions, levelled our weapons at the harbour entrance and waited for the vessel to enter. The boat rounded the mole and nosed its way into the harbour. Once it had turned itself about and was lying parallel with the harbour wall, it was plain to see that it was one of ours. This was confirmed when we saw the white ensign that flew from the stern. This was obviously our taxi.

We rushed on to the jetty and greeted the crew of the gunboat, a fine bunch of sailors, who cheerfully assisted with the loading of our canoes and our not inconsiderable cargo of stores, weapons, and explosives. With everything stowed the skipper made ready to leave. Soon we were heading out into the open sea.

Chapter 6

Chios and Naxos

The gunboat, with us on board, was expected to patrol the Aegean sea, and eventually make its way to the island of Chios. It had been reported that the Germans had evacuated this island, and we were to verify this report. We marines were to effect a landing, and search for any sign of current enemy activity.

During our time on patrol we hoped we could avoid any encounter with an E-boat since our small craft would stand no chance whatsoever against one. Darkness fell and with it came bigger seas. The boat began to dip and roll, and we hoped that we were not in for one of the storms, notorious in these parts, that just whip up from nowhere. Our little craft would not fare too well against such hostility. With nowhere immediately accessible to take refuge, we could only hope to ride out whatever came our way.

Despite our prayers the storm paid us a visit, tossing our small craft about like a cork. Somehow the little boat managed to cut a path through the rolling sea. There was very limited space below so we were taking shelter on the upper deck, which although crowded was made easier with the issue of our rum ration. Now we were with the Navy we were entitled to the customary tot. It's amazing how a little alcohol can make everything seem more bearable. Enough and one's perspective can change quite considerably. The cold and wet did not seem to matter so much.

All through the night we tossed and rolled. Only by the skilled seamanship of the crew was the vessel kept afloat. Huge waves broke over the bow of our tiny craft, and occasionally as the skipper altered course in an attempt to combat the conditions, a massive wave would catch us broadside; it was a miracle we didn't capsize.

The following morning, instead of dawn bringing with it a calmer sea, as is often the case, the storm worsened to such an extent that the captain decided to seek shelter somewhere among the islands. Pitching and rolling, we skirted a small island until the skipper spotted a tiny cove that he thought could accommodate a boat of our size.

Skilfully the skipper manoeuvred the craft into the refuge, where thankfully the waters were much calmer. We dropped anchor and set about getting a meal on the go. It was amazing, despite the rough conditions, our bodies wanted food; I was starving. With luck we could stay in this haven until the storm subsided. The ship's cook was nothing short of a wizard, the way he managed to conjure up 'scran' (Navy for grub) for everyone on board. Even more remarkable was that the fellow's main job afloat was a specialist aircraft spotter. It would not be long before this skill would also be put to the test.

We were tucking into our meal when with a roar and a swoosh, a fighter plane swooped down on us. It took us completely by surprise. We dropped plates of food and dived to man the guns. My allotted task on this boat was to man the twin Vickers machine gun, but before I could swing the gun's barrels into a position where they would be effective the plane was out of range, dipping and skimming across the waves and heading out to sea. However, before any of us could identify the aircraft, and relax, it banked sharply, and headed, wave-top high, straight at us.

We called for our cook/spotter to identify the fighter, before we opened up on it. Much to our relief our spotter took no time at all to declare it friendly. Although we had all the armament available to us trained on the fighter, had it been hostile we were a sitting target. All we now hoped was that the plane's observer was as competent as ours had been, and would spot the white ensign we flew. Thankfully he was, and the pilot pulled the aircraft up sharply and climbed over the cliffs behind us, flying out of sight.

The scare over, we settled once more to finish what was left of our grub. Much to the matelots' pleasure the marines had volunteered to share watch-keeping duties (here I go again, my old dad told me never to volunteer for anything). I was allocated the first part of the middle watch. That is to say from midnight until two o'clock.

Although the days were rather pleasant, by contrast the nights were bitterly cold. Staring out in the inky blackness your eyes played tricks on you. I saw a German E-boat that turned into a battleship which in turn turned into a fleet of ships. It would have been easy to sound the alarm and have everyone on board rush to their battle stations. But when they found out there was no danger, I would have been none too popular with anyone. I was thankful when my duty came to an end, and a colleague relieved me. I thought it prudent not to mention the 'ships' I had 'seen'.

Next morning waking to the customary 'gunfire' (mug of tea) we were all pretty anxious to observe the weather conditions. Although the storm had died somewhat there was still quite a bit of swell. Our skipper was happy enough with the conditions and gave the order to weigh anchor. With engines throbbing the little boat nosed its way out of the cove and into the open sea. It was decided to hug the shoreline of the island we were leaving, then whilst still shrouded by shadow from the towering landscape, make a dash for the island nearest to us. Before we could do this one of our lookouts signalled enemy ahead. Sure enough in the distance was the unmistakable wake of an E-boat. We hugged the coastline even tighter, steering around the headland as fast as our little boat could go. Two marines were landed on the shore and detailed to climb the cliff and report on the movements of the E-boat. Fortunately for us the E-boat was observed disappearing over the horizon without spotting us.

Our nine lives were ebbing away. With the two marines safely back on board we steamed toward the island of Chios.

Early next day we sighted Chios. With feelings of apprehension we closed on our objective. Although the island had been reported as safe, it was always possible the enemy might have left a token force there. Proceeding with the utmost caution with everyone at battle stations, we nosed our way towards the harbour entrance. To our surprise, on the distant jetty, a crowd had gathered and they were waving to us. Although we were still too far away positively to identify the nationality of the people waving, we thought it hardly seemed likely that they were Germans.

We nosed our way through the entrance of the tiny harbour and tied up alongside the wall. We marines, armed with sub-machine guns, leapt ashore. Within minutes, we were surrounded by a crowd of cheering backslapping Greeks, who assured us there were no Germans on the island. Even the resistance fighters had come down from the hills and were enjoying their newly found freedom.

The captain of the little gunboat had a few words with our CO and together they decided it might be more prudent to move around to the north side of the island. Assuring our Greek friends that we were not going far, we cast off and made way. It took about half an hour to steam to the north side, where we arrived in a small bay. An advance party of marines was landed to check the situation. We had not gone far, when once again Greeks mobbed us, this time mainly children. The locals informed us that, although the Germans had left, during their occupation they had kept the islanders very short of food and had also committed a number of atrocities.

We were concerned for these poor people and wondered what we could do about the food situation. Our boat carried only sufficient for the needs of the crew and us marines. The cook dug out a tin of biscuits that were really only to be used in an emergency. They were of the hard tack variety that needed soaking before being edible. However, we tore the tin open and offered them to the swarms of children who were now surrounding us intent on grabbing anything on offer. One tiny lad, not wanting to miss out, dived his hand into the tin and grabbed a packet of biscuits. As he withdrew his hand his thin little arm was laid bare by the ragged edge of the tin. We tried to grab hold of him but he fought like a tiger. We eventually managed to subdue him, treat his wound, and wrap a field dressing around his arm. Despite all this activity, at no time did the lad let go of the packet of biscuits he was clutching!

A few days passed before we received a message ordering us back to the island's main harbour, saying vessels of our fleet had arrived and that Chios, although some 120 miles behind the enemy front line, was now declared a base. The 'vessels of the fleet' consisted of a motor torpedo boat, and a small submarine! A medic and engineers of the SAS HQ staff had also arrived on the island.

We found suitable premises in which to live, each quickly laying claim to his space. The entire village was enclosed by barbed wire, which had been put there by the Germans, in a bid to deter the resistance fighters. The enemy had also booby trapped the area, making it extremely dangerous to go anywhere near the wire. After careful inspection we eventually did manage to negotiate safe passage through, which enabled us to patrol.

During one of our forays through the wire, a small box was

spotted. It had just broken the surface and was clearly visible. Having been told, quite emphatically, not to touch anything we thought suspicious we reported the find to our engineer, who began to crawl forward to get a closer look at the box. On reaching the object the engineer called to us that it was in fact a booby-trap device and that he would attempt to disarm it.

We watched at a safe distance as with the utmost care the engineer began to remove the earth from around the device. All seemed to be going well when a violent explosion shook us. A cloud of dust and smoke enveloped the brave sapper. As he had tried to lift the device the booby-trap sprung, blowing off both the poor man's arms. For a few seconds we stood, dumbfounded, then the awful truth hit us. As one, we ran forward, only to be met by a barked order from the medic to hold hard. Of course this was good sense we could have all been killed by such carelessness.

The medic, whom up until now we had considered to be a bit of a softie, immediately showed us his real worth. On his belly, he quickly crawled forward until he had reached the engineer then, like the professional he was, he administered first aid. He plunged a shot of morphine into the casualty, then dressed his terrible wounds. Then, still surrounded by booby traps, he dragged his patient back through the wire. As soon as we were able, we helped the medic transfer the wounded man to a torpedo boat, which swiftly carried him to Egypt. This incident increased our bitterness toward the enemy, and taught us to be extremely careful in future – especially when treading where our enemies had already trodden.

Brigadier Turnbull the officer in charge of all raiding forces in the Aegean now joined us on Chios. This confirmed the thoughts we harboured that the enemy would not be likely to try to re-occupy this particular island. Our new commander didn't take long in finding us a job. Seeing as we were the only marines in the vicinity, and with no immediate operations in view, the brigadier thought we could fill the role of policemen. We didn't mind our new appointment, although it did lead to a number of altercations with the freedom fighters, now located in the village, and determined to drink the wine cellars dry. There were a few busted heads on both sides.

The days lingered, then one morning, our CO awakened me and said I was to prepare for an operation. My spirits perked up a bit, as I thought of what might lie ahead. In a positive frame of mind I hastily gathered my kit together and made my way down to the harbour as instructed. On approaching the jetty I could see that the harbour was filled with caiques, making ready to sail. Waiting to board were a number of soldiers of the Greek Sacred Squadron, the equivalent of our SAS, who were operating with our forces in the Aegean.

As I made to board one of the caiques, I was introduced to a captain of the SAS, who informed me that I was to be his aide. The aim of the operation we were embarking upon was to liberate the island of Naxos. Intelligence had informed us that the enemy soldiers there were so fed up with their lot, that as soon as we put in a show they would undoubtedly surrender without fuss. We heard this a number of times, but never did we encounter any such apathy among the foe.

My main job was to keep in communication with a small gun-boat on which a fellow marine would be receiving, and responding to my messages. With everyone at their stations the small flotilla headed out from the harbour into the open sea. Soon we were on course for Naxos. I had no idea what kind of terrain we would encounter on the island, but with a heavy radio set strapped to my back, prayed that there would not be too much climbing. We sailed through the night, and as the sun pierced the morning sky, my dreams were shattered by the sight of huge cliffs rising looming ahead. I thought 'Bloody hell, how am I going to lug my kit up there with a cumbersome radio set on my back'.

It was still quite dark as we jumped over the side of the vessels into the knee-deep surf. Soon we were on the shore and scaling the cliff. When I looked around and saw the amount of kit and ammu-nition the Greek lads had to carry, suddenly my gear didn't feel so heavy. In no time, and much to my own surprise, I was at the top of the cliff.

The Germans were encamped in what appeared to be an old castle, and it would be difficult to dislodge them. From positions of cover we aimed every weapon we had at the enemy, and waited for the sun to put in a full appearance. In daylight it was easy to see the enemy positions and, on the command, every weapon we had opened up to rake the enemy encampment. We kept up the barrage for a full minute, then ceased firing. After the crescendo, the stillness was eerie. We hoisted a white flag signalling that hostilities should cease, and we should talk. Thankfully the enemy understood the message, and likewise raised their flag of peace.

Cautiously, and following close behind my captain, who fortunately could speak German fluently, so there should be no misunderstanding, we entered 'no man's land' and were relieved to see two Germans walking towards us. We came to a halt a respectable distance apart and, on discovering that the German officer now standing opposite us could speak excellent English, my captain insisted that we conduct negotiations in our native tongue; the German accepted this without fuss. I was very grateful for this, since I could neither understand nor speak any German, and it was my job to communicate with the gunboat.

My officer, Captain Hillman, suggested to the Germans that as the war was almost at an end, and since we had landed in force, it would be a tragedy to waste any more young German blood, and that they should surrender their garrison to us. This was a tremendous game of bluff, since there were only forty Greek soldiers ashore, whilst the enemy garrison amounted to some 200 or more. The garrison commander was not easily taken in, and asked what the strength of our force was. Needless to say there was no way would we have disclosed this whatever our strength might have been. Captain Hillman calmly assured the German that we had more than sufficient troops to storm his bastion should he decide to fight on.

The enemy officer pondered for a while, then pointing at my cap badge, said he was willing to surrender his troops to the Royal Marines, supposing we could produce enough to convince him. My officer responded saying that, although the marine he was addressing was the only one in view, there were a good deal more close enough to summon by radio. This did little to convince our enemy, who said he wanted to see for himself sufficient numbers of marines to encourage his surrender. We pointed out that we did in fact have a big enough force of Greek soldiers to overrun his stronghold. To this the German officer replied indignantly, that he would never surrender to a Greek contingent. The captain tried a different method of persuasion, asking the enemy if they would surrender to the Navy. The German commander readily agreed, providing the ship was large enough to impress him. Once more our bluff had not worked.

We saluted one another, turned about and marched back to our own lines. Our hopes for an early end to the conflict had failed, we would have to fight on and rout the enemy in order to liberate the island. Once back in the cover of our lines, I relayed what had taken place to my opposite number on the gunboat. The skipper of the little boat decided to try his own bluff and, although he had been told it was fruitless, steamed into the bay. My radio fell silent as all hands on the boat prepared for action. Suddenly the sound of rapid fire from the Bofors guns on the gunboat filled the air. I ran to the top of a ridge to get a look at what was happening, to see a German seaplane trying to take off. The gunboat poured round after round of ammo into the plane riddling it like a pepper pot. To the credit of the pilot, and 'the rub of the green' the seaplane managed to get airborne and with trails of gunsmoke in its wake, disappeared over the horizon.

By no means disheartened, the gunboat skipper steered his small craft into the harbour, hoping the sight of a naval vessel might convince the German garrison commander to see sense. We held our breath, and waited to see what the reception would be. We didn't have to wait long before all hell let loose. The Germans opened fire with everything they had, bringing down an intense barrage onto the gunboat. Now it was the turn of the gunboat to call on lady luck, and she responded with kindness. The gunboat was able to make a swift exit from the harbour and steam out of range of enemy gunfire without suffering any damage or casualties.

By now we realized that the enemy was intercepting our radio signals, and I was told to break off all contact with the gunboat. Then our SAS captain thought he would try another bluff. He told me to contact the gunboat and ask when we could expect the RAF, not thinking for one moment that the air force had any planes spare to support us. Fortunately for us the skipper of the boat took the message seriously.

We began to exchange fire with the enemy. Mortar bombs were falling all around us. The enemy had our range, and the situation was getting pretty grim. To withdraw from the island was out of the question. We would just have to sit tight and hope, that come nightfall, we could move up closer to the garrison, enabling an assault to be made. Then, above the sound of gunfire, we could hear an aircraft engine. At first I wondered was it ours, or, thinking the escaping seaplane might have reported the situation on the island, was it the enemy coming to the rescue of the garrison? Suddenly three aircraft flew into view and began circling over our heads. We lay on the ground looking skywards trying to recognize the planes. What a relief it was when we could see that they were rocket-armed Beaufighters, some of the very latest planes the Royal Air Force had. The first plane picked out his target, then with a waggle of his wings, to let us know he knew our positions, the pilot made his low level run. The 'Whump' of the first rocket strike was soon followed by another mighty thud, as two missiles tore through the garrison wall.

We had a grandstand view as the second of the Beaufighters approached the target at low level, and as his comrade before him, with the enemy pouring everything they had at the incoming aircraft, he fired his rockets. Now there was a gaping great hole in the enemy's defences. The third Beaufighter followed the same procedure opening up more gaps in the garrison wall. Not content with unloading their rockets on the enemy, the three Beaufighters banked, and returned, raking the garrison walls with machine-gun fire.

This was our cue to move up. The Greek soldiers were as keen as mustard to get at the enemy; the Sacred Squadron had hearts as big as lions'. In no time we were at the gates, smashing them down, and pouring into the enemy compound. We met very little resistance, and as we broke through the complex, with the fight pretty much drained out of them, the Germans laid down their weapons, surrendering with as much dignity as we afforded them. We lined up our prisoners in the courtyard, and thought we had accounted for everyone who had been in the garrison. Then we noticed that in fact the garrison commander was conspicuous by his absence, and decided to go and look for him.

A small group of us raced through the empty corridors of the castle, kicking open doors and jumping into rooms, pistols at the ready, just in case he was waiting, and hoping to take a few of us with him. A pistol shot echoed through a passageway, it seemed to have come from a room at the far end. We ran to the end of the passage, and in the classic style, two each side of the door, without ceremony, kicked it open. The commander was sprawled across his desk, a Luger pistol still in his hand. He had blown the top of his head off. He had really been determined not to surrender. Back in the courtyard we detailed four German soldiers to collect the body of their commander, and bring him out, so that he could be laid to rest in a manner that befitted a soldier, and a brave man.

Our next task was to get the prisoners away from the island. Most were subdued and looked thoroughly beaten, but some still bore a look of arrogance. The locals were not too happy with their past captors and vented their feelings as we passed. The only way we could evacuate the prisoners was by sea, and the only transport we had was the little gunboat. There was nothing for it, we had to commandeer the caiques, and their respective crews, herd all the prisoners on board and set sail.

Soon a small flotilla was at sea, and from the gunboat I looked back on a liberated island. An extremely successful operation – at last I could dump this bloody wireless set!

Chapter 7

Capturing a General?

Once we were secured alongside the jetty of Chios, Captain Hillman and I stepped off the gunboat. I bid farewell to my naval friends and rejoined my fellow marines, who were still carrying out their duties as policemen. It was great to be back with my buddies again and enjoy the good-natured banter that passed between us.

After the liberation of Naxos, and before a week had passed, I was woken from my sleep and told to report to the jetty where I would be briefed. On arriving at the jetty, instead of the jostling caiques making ready for sea, everything was surprisingly quiet, with just one boat manned by a British Navy crew making ready. As I stood by, a marine who introduced himself as Turfrey, sidled up to me saying he was to accompany me on the forthcoming 'do', whatever it might be.

I was not exactly jumping for joy at the prospect of going on a mission with the marine standing before me. This would be his first operation and to have to take a novice on a mission, which was obviously of a covert nature, seemed a trifle unfair on me. I know we all have to experience our first operation, but when we do, it's generally among a number of experienced men, and not just one! I thought I had better wait and see what the mission was all about before pre-judging the suitability of my companion.

The CO approached, and we were soon in conversation. He informed me that I was to be taken by a caique to the vicinity of the island of Fournoi, where together with the other marine we were to launch a canoe and paddle to the island. Fournoi is due south of Chios, and was reputed to have a radar station. Once on the island our job would be to go to ground and report any enemy activity. We were to stay on Fournoi for three days, and make notes in preparation for a raid that was planned to destroy the radio/radar installations. The caique, manned by British sailors, would return and rendezvous with us on the evening of the third day, supposing of course that we had not been captured, or shot. I didn't see much point in sharing with my CO the reservations I had about my colleague. But I did hope the marine would show his mettle.

As we boarded the caique I could see that my canoe was already loaded and it was a comfort to see my old friend again. I hadn't used it since arriving in the Aegean. I gave a cheerful wave to those on the jetty, and with my number two by my side prepared to settle down for the journey.

It was a lovely evening, with the sea flat calm as we sailed towards the target area. Both Turfrey and I offered to take our turn on watch, but the sailors would have none of it, reminding us that our job would be on us soon enough. They were a terrific bunch of lads. So, with only time to kill, we fell into a deep sleep.

Next morning we woke to a welcome cup of tea, steaming hot it was too. I talked with the coxswain, a petty officer, and he assured me that we were on course and with time on our side we should reach our setting down point by evening. It was a serene day, the sea was still calm and the sun shone on us from a near cloudless sky. The warmth from the sun and the gentle movement of the boat made for a most relaxing cruise. It was as though we hadn't a care in the world, and apart from occasionally scanning the horizon for the dreaded E-boats, we had little to worry about. Currently, the enemy's E-boats were conspicuous by their absence. Whether that was due to our Navy recently drafting in a number of fast and superior gunboats, I didn't know. We hadn't seen sight of an E-boat for quite a while. Whatever the reason, we weren't missing them one bit!

Soon it was dusk, and then darkness enveloped us. The coxswain summoned me to the wheelhouse, pointed to a large blob on the horizon, and said, 'That's Fournoi, dead ahead of us son.' I continued to watch from my position in the wheelhouse as the caique closed on the island. At no more than a crawl and without making any undue noise, the skipper cruised around the island looking for a suitable place that we could make for after launching. As we were rounding the north end of the island the coxswain spied a small cove and asked me if it would do. I said it looked perfect. With the engines of the boat barely turning over, the caique nosed its way into the harbour. Straining my eyes and peering through the darkness all seemed quiet, in fact too bloody quiet for my liking. Becoming suspicious, in a whisper I confided my feelings to the coxswain, who readily agreed.

Still scanning the dark contours of the land, which I estimated to be about three hundred yards distant, and unable to detect any sign of activity I made my decision and told coxswain, 'Right, let's go.' The boat's anchor was dropped and the young matelots quickly lowered my canoe over the side. The old fishing boat now quite still, I climbed over the side and into the front of my trusty friend. Turfrey, soon climbed in behind me. With our equipment and weapons already on board, all that was left was for the sailors to hand down our rations and water, enough for three days.

Gently I pushed the bow of the canoe away from the side of the caique, then, in tandem, my partner and I paddled stealthily towards the shore. I was still apprehensive about my number two, and my mind flashed back to that night in December 1942, when, as our canoe came alongside the first ship we were to attack in Bordeaux harbour, without any warning, we were bathed in light from the powerful torch of a deck sentry. We froze, and my mind raced. Would my partner be able to hold his nerve, and would I? I was convinced that I could hold out, but to me the man in front was an unknown factor; for that matter he could be thinking the same of me.

This being my number two's initiation, and given the circumstances, I don't think I could be blamed for being a trifle tense. My life depended upon him keeping his nerve in an emergency, though, in fairness, thus far he was showing no sign of anxiety whatsoever.

The silhouette of the island was now defined and this enabled us to keep a steady line as we made our approach. Turning my head I could see the old caique gently swaying at anchor, knowing full well that she would leave swiftly if the occasion demanded it.

The bows of our canoe slid up the beach as we came to a halt. For a moment we remained still with eyes wide open looking for any sign of activity. Then, cautiously, I climbed out of the canoe and dragged it further up the beach to enable my number two to alight without getting too wet. Together, we swiftly carried the canoe into some bushes, and covered it with a camouflage net in the hope it would not come to the attention of any prying eyes. At this stage we just stood silently, not even speaking in a whisper. Using my torch, I signalled to the caique that we had landed safely. I heard the engines start up, then using the very minimum of power, the boat turned and headed out of the little bay. I felt somewhat alone – discarded.

I still had a feeling of uneasiness; it was just too quiet. Gradually my eyes became more accustomed to the darkness and I scanned the hills immediately behind us. Returning to inspect the beach once more my heart missed a beat and I froze. Up ahead, tucked away in among some bushes, I could clearly see what looked to me like the shape of a pillbox. I nudged Turfrey, he jumped slightly, then nodded in awareness. My mind was racing, had they seen us land? It so, why had they not attacked? I tried to understand the enemy, and their reasons for allowing us to come ashore unmolested, but it was no good, it just didn't make any sense.

I figured there could be only one solution, namely the lookouts in the pillbox must be asleep. To lie where we were and wait for daylight was not an option. Something had to be done.

I suddenly realized that it was up to me; it was my decision, and mine alone. I crept closer to my companion, and, whispering in his ear, told him of my plan. I was going to creep along the beach and try to establish whether or not the box was manned. My colleague nodded in agreement. I slid onto the beach and began to crawl like a snake. My back felt naked and I thought anyone looking would see me easily. Slowly, painfully slowly, I got nearer to the pillbox, and still there was no sign of life. At times like this the urge to get up and run forward is immense, but you dare not. Stick to your training, be patient and stay low. The minutes seemed like hours as I closed on the enemy; there was still no sound as I crawled around to the entrance. I had decided that, if the strongpoint was manned, I would throw myself at the entrance and lob a grenade in amongst the occupants. I mused, 'If they are asleep, that should wake the buggers up!' I reached the entrance and once more the training kicked in, I stood flush against the outer wall and listened. No sound could I hear. I thought, hoped, that it was empty. With my pistol in my left hand and a grenade in my right I slid through the entrance, thankfully my gut instinct proved sound, the pillbox was in fact unoccupied.

Now the mystery deepened. Why would a strongpoint at the most vulnerable part of the island remain unmanned? With the aid of my torch I surveyed the empty pillbox. Although there was nothing of value to us, it was obvious by the mess they had left behind them that the occupants evacuated in a hurry. I went outside and signalled to my companion to join me. Jointly, we decided that it would be safer to spend the rest of the night in the vacated pillbox than on the open beach. However, we couldn't afford to become complacent, so took turns to keep watch. At least we managed a little welcome shuteye.

As dawn broke over a shimmering sea, I informed my colleague that it was time to move and find a position from where we could observe any sign of enemy activity. Laden down by our kit and stores, slowly we began to climb the hills and make our way to where we had been informed the enemy positions lay. I was looking out across the bay when I began thinking that perhaps I was hallucinating, for there on the horizon and steaming straight towards us was a destroyer. I thought, 'It can't be', we had put what destroyers the enemy had in the Aegean out of action.

As the sun rose I could see quite clearly that with the destroyer was what looked to me to be a cruiser. Other vessels were now coming into view and, one of them I was sure was a carrier. I turned to my fellow marine, to ask what he made of it, and he said that he was as bemused as I was. Then the sound of an aircraft engine brought us back to reality. The plane it came from swooped on us from the sea and strafed the ridge on which we were standing with machine-gun fire. The pilot was trying to draw our attention to the fact that we should not be there – he certainly wasn't trying to hit us. That he could have done quite easily. Frantically we waved to him in recognition, and he waggled his wings and veered away. Up until this moment we still thought that the enemy occupied the island and that the incoming fleet was hostile. It transpired that the Navy had in fact been here before us, and after giving the enemy positions a battering with their guns, had landed a detachment of marines. The enemy, after a token skirmish, had been only too pleased to give up the struggle.

At this point I decided we should proceed to the main town on the island and identify ourselves. We were strolling casually along the cliff path, still fascinated by the build-up of warships in the bay, when a burst of machine-gun fire swept over our heads. We hit the deck. Wouldn't you have? Recognizing the unmistakable sound as coming from a British Army Bren gun, the gun must have been fired, I reasoned, by a British soldier. Dodging behind some rocks, I answered the challenge the only way I knew a Tommy would recognize, with a burst of colourful language identifiable as definitely coming from a boot-neck. Standing in clear view of us our would-be assailant laughingly confirmed that he could have got us if he had chosen to. I didn't doubt it for a moment.

Together, we walked down from the hill and into the town where, on the beach, our Navy was evacuating the remains of the German garrison. For them 'the war was over' as they were fond of saying to our lads when they took them prisoner earlier in the conflict. Now it was their turn to spend the duration of the hostilities in a POW camp somewhere.

I presented myself to the marine officer in charge of the landing party and introduced my comrade too. The officer was astounded that we had landed on the island alone, and said he never expected to meet two black-faced bandits. He offered us a lift back to base, which sadly we had to decline. Firstly, their base would be in Alexandria, whilst we were due back on Chios. And, secondly, what about the rescue party; they were due to come and take us off the island in three days? If we didn't show they might think we had been captured, or worse, killed. After saying farewell, Turfrey and I made our way back to the pillbox to wait for the caique that had brought us to this island.

As we retraced our way along the cliff tops we had the opportunity to witness the damage caused by the onslaught of our navy. They had left very little standing, and there were signs of a hasty retreat. German helmets and equipment lay scattered everywhere and one could only imagine the panic that must have ensued when the first of the British Navy's heavy salvos rained down on the enemy positions.

Back in the pillbox we prepared for a long wait, and pondered on what we could do to occupy our time. After eating our meagre compact rations, we decided to get some shuteye. The ground we lay curled up on was cold and hard and slumber was difficult, so after a while I decided to go down to the beach, now in darkness, and sit there. As I looked out across the water, with the waves gently lapping the shore and the stillness of night, the war and old London seemed such a long way off.

My eyes now fully accustomed to the dark, I thought I could make out the shape of a vessel feeling its way into the bay. I concentrated on the movement of the shape, then considering it could be the enemy, I signalled to my colleague to join me, and together we got ourselves into a position of defence. I had reasoned that perhaps the Germans were hoping to pick up any survivors who might have escaped the invasion of the island by our troops.

As the craft drew closer I identified it as a small caique, similar to the one we were waiting for. The boat stopped in the middle of the bay and dropped anchor. I watched to see if a small boat was lowered over the side. Then came a signal from a torch, which I recognized. It flashed briefly, confirming this was in fact our transport off the island. I returned the signal then, with my mate close behind me, raced to where we had stowed our canoe. We gathered our gear as fast as we could and dragged the canoe down to the waters edge, pushing into the gentle surf without delay. As we paddled out to the caique, it struck me as odd that our rescuers had come to collect us two days before they were due.

Once alongside, friendly sailors whispering 'thank goodness we found you' greeted us, then with eager hands pulled both canoe and men over the side of the boat. 'Why all the whispering?', I asked. 'In case the enemy on shore are listening,' came the hushed reply. The coxswain said he had noticed a lot of ships in the distance, and immediately thought them hostile. He thought that the enemy might be intending to reinforce the island and, if that was their intention, considered our predicament, so came early in the hope of effecting a rescue. I thanked him and shook his hand warmly. What grand chaps these Navy lads were. I explained what had taken place on the island, and somewhat relieved, the officer responded by ordering the engines to be started.

No longer protected by the shelter from the island we encountered a stiff breeze, and then it started to rain. As the sea became more violent the bows of the boat dipped into the troughs ahead, so we altered course, but the heavy seas met us broadside, and the vessel lurched dangerously. The storm now raged and huge waves broke over the side. The boat was being swamped. All hands frantically bailed, with every receptacle they could find to fill. Furiously we emptied the contents of our makeshift bailing utensils back into the briny. I began to think we were losing the battle, and wondered if in fact the little boat could stand such a battering. The situation was serious.

The Aegean sea is dotted with dozens of small islands, some so insignificant they were not named on our charts. We had steered quite close to one of these no-name islands, and sensibly the skipper hugged its coastline. The storm was winning and our boat was lying precariously low in the water. I thought that at any moment we would have to abandon ship, but not in the least did I fancy the prospect. Our chances of survival in the raging sea would have been minimal. With great skill, the skipper managed to keep the boat afloat and steered it around the northern tip of the island, where he hoped to find the sea a little calmer. Quite unexpectedly, and to our pleasant surprise, we came upon a sheltered bay, if we could just keep afloat long enough to make it to this welcoming sanctuary.

With great dexterity the skipper managed to coax the caique into the bay, and although we were in calmer waters at last, it was too late to save the old fishing vessel. The last swell as we entered the shelter of the bay had been too much for the gallant little boat and she began to sink. The shout went up 'every man for himself' and we leapt into the water and swam for the shore, which, thankfully, was only a short distance away. Our strength had been sapped by the struggle with the elements, so we crawled up the beach and lay down. Soon most of us were asleep.

We awoke to the pleasant warmth of the sun, the storm had abated, and all was calm once more. Everything looked glorious until reality took over; how would we get off this island? Only the bows of the caique were still visible, sticking proudly above a now gentle sea. It was decided to swim out to the wreck to see what could be salvaged; some of our rations we hoped. Three of us made the swim and luckily found a few tins stowed in the bow. Some contained meat pudding and others corned beef. Then to our surprise and great joy we found, intact, the ship's stock of Navy rum – 'Corn in Egypt'. Quite naturally, for Navy and marines alike, this booty now took priority. We emerged from the sea and struggled back up the beach. As soon as the rest of the lads caught sight of the grog we were carrying, they greeted us like bloomin' heroes. Now, if we didn't get rescued, we wouldn't care a sod, and at least we would die happy!

We were sitting on the sand, quite content, when over the brow of a nearby hill a figure appeared. The Greek, a native of the island on which we were 'shipwrecked' approached and told us that he had heard of our plight in the village; how, we will never know.

The man then informed us that there were two caiques moored in the island's harbour. The Germans were using the boats and their Greek crews had no alternative but to obey their oppressors for fear of reprisals against their families. However, the local man continued, the crew would be quite happy to be captured by the British.

Here was our means of escape from the island, and made more attractive, by the assurance that currently there were no enemy troops around to stop us. We agreed, to the delight of our informant, that we would 'capture' the two boats. The Greek volunteered to lead us to the harbour, but only after insisting that he take us first to a monastery in the hills for a blessing. It was a reasonable enough request, so there seemed little point in refusing.

Marines and matelots followed the guide over the first hill where two more Greeks met us with donkeys. Straddled on one of the donkeys, I was soon jogging along a rough and winding path leading up to a monastery. On reaching the holy place we were greeted by a monk, whom we understood to be the top man, and invited to come inside the chapel. We knelt side-by-side whilst the holy man blessed us.

Duly blessed we offered our gratitude and bade farewell. Astride my donkey once more and with my feet almost touching the ground, we began our descent. These marvellous little animals were so surefooted, we were down the hill in no time, much quicker than walking I assure you. We must have looked a motley bunch as, led by our guide, we entered the village intent on taking possession of our sea transport. The villagers greeted us as liberators and rang bells, then offered wine. In generous quantities, too! However, much to the obvious disappointment of the villagers, we had to decline their hospitality. It was necessary that we concentrate on the task in hand. The crews of the two caiques came to greet us, smiling and with the usual slap on the back, they said how grateful they were to be liberated. Eagerly, we boarded the boats and directed the skippers to take us to the north of the island, to pick up the remaining sailors.

When we arrived in the north the waiting sailors were so pleased to see us with transport sufficient to take the lot of us off the island, that their petty officer suggested we splice the main-brace, a celebration I readily agreed with. We were fortunate indeed, as after losing one boat we had now 'found' two!

70

Our guide told us of a neighbouring island not too far away occupied by an Italian garrison, a force of seven men. I asked him if he would take us there and he readily agreed. As well as my fellow marine, Turfrey, I chose a young naval stoker to accompany us on our mission to capture the enemy. I was pretty confident that we could capture seven Italians. We boarded our new caique and headed out of the bay.

We arrived on the island in bright sunlight, and slipped ashore. With our Greek guide in the lead, we set foot along the track that would lead to the village where the garrison was situated. As we walked, we passed some isolated houses and to our surprise their occupants came out to wave and cheer us. Nice, but I hoped this did not signal that the 'bush telegraph' we were now coming to recognize, was working as well on this island as it had been on the one we had just left. I didn't fancy being ambushed one bit.

At some length, we arrived on the edge of the village and found all was quiet. Our guide pointed out a large corner house, saying it was where the Italian soldiers were billeted. I surveyed the situation and decided to tell Turfrey and the sailor to fire at the windows, whilst I would run forward and kick the door in. Once I was inside I instructed them to follow me in as fast as they could. My comrades took up their positions, I gave the nod, and they opened up on the windows, the young sailor fulfilling his desire to fire a Tommy gun. Under the cover of their fire I ran forward and aimed my boot at the door; it opened with ease. These Italians had not even considered the possibility that they might be in danger from the enemy, so they hadn't even bothered to secure the door. As I ran up the stairs I was aware that my comrades were close behind me. It was a good feeling. Entering the first room we encountered six Italian soldiers already standing with their arms above their heads in surrender. We quickly gathered up their weapons and herded them into a corner of the room. Then it struck me, our guide had said there were seven men, if that were so, then where was the seventh?

Hurriedly, I mounted the second flight of stairs, and with my pistol cocked and levelled, burst into the first room I came to. There, sitting on a bunk and crying like a baby, was the missing man. I felt sorry for him. Terribly afraid, he was shaking like a leaf. I motioned him to stand, and when he did I gasped at what I saw. His tunic would have put that of a lion tamer to shame! The gold braid was fantastic, and his riding britches had a three-inch gold stripe running down the legs. On his feet were the grandest pair of leather boots I had seen in a long while. Relieving the Italian of his revolver, I bade him put on his cap, on which an embroidered badge stretched from ear to ear. I was convinced I had captured a high-ranking officer, a general at least. I could see the headlines emblazoned across all the daily papers, 'Marine captures Italian general'. I was determined to take good care of my prisoner on the trip back to base, where I was sure my boss would be delighted with my trophy.

Telling 'Tony' (the name I had given my prisoner) that his war was over, I ushered him down the stairs where the others were waiting. With 'Tony' at the head we marched our prisoners into the street. I quite expected a feeling of jubilation among the locals, instead of the silence that greeted us. Apparently the islanders had become friendly with the Italians, who, unlike the Germans, their partners in crime, had treated them well. With the locals waving farewell, we marched our prisoners down to the beach and escorted them aboard the waiting caiques. Because they were only seven in number, I thought they would probably be found work back at our base.

Chapter 8

Milos and The Sacred Squadron

En route to Chios we had to pass the island of Samos, where we had heard there was some fighting. The Greek Sacred Squadron had landed intending to liberate the island, but were meeting with stiff opposition from German troops. We decided to pay them a visit to see if in some way we could help their cause.

The Sacred Squadron had been formed in December 1942, in Palestine as part of the SAS. Its commanding officer was Colonel Christodoulos Tsigantes. The officers and men were volunteers, most of them having escaped from Greece at the time of the German invasion. They included members of all three branches of the Greek armed forces as well as officers of the gendarmerie and the coast guard. In the beginning the squadron's strength was limited to about 200 men. Later it increased to around 1,100. The soldiers of the Sacred Squadron were trained for unorthodox operations – desert warfare, parachuting, close-order-combat, demolition and activities involving boats and sea-borne raiding.

From March 1944 until May 1945 the squadron carried out many raiding operations on the Dodecanese islands under the command of Brigadier Turnbull. The object of their missions was to wear the enemy down by causing losses of both personnel and equipment. Operating from remote land bases they effected surprise attacks, mostly sea-borne, creating havoc during which they captured sentries and patrols and pinned down enemy forces.

The Sacred Squadron played the principal role in liberating the Aegean and Dodecanese islands and it was also the deciding factor in reuniting the latter with their motherland. The presence of the Squadron in this strategic area and its struggles manifested the indisputable rights of Greece to territories which have been hers

73

since ancient times and which rights are, unfortunately, disputed by certain of her neighbours. These disputers, during the Second World War, elected to remain as simply spectators or, worse, sided with the forces of Fascism or Nazism.

I never fought with more loyal and courageous men.

We entered the Bay of Samos and expected to hear gunfire, but there was none. As we came alongside the jetty cheering crowds gathered. They had convinced themselves that with a British boat in their harbour surely they must now be liberated. We were surprised to see a number of freedom fighters among the people, and wondered why they were not in the hills where we thought the fighting must be, helping their brothers.

We climbed onto the jetty to be greeted with the usual back-slapping, coming mainly from freedom fighters, who were always eager to be first to greet us. We were invited to go to the homes of a few locals and partake of the local brew. We had already sunk a few tots of rum on our voyage, so by the time we added a measure or two of the local stuff I for one was feeling a bit light-headed. When one of the local dignitaries explained that there was an un-exploded bomb in the vicinity, and asked could we do some thing about it. I readily volunteered to take a look.

We were led to a small clearing on the outskirts of the village and shown a 500lb bomb partly buried. I estimated that there was about three feet of the thing above ground. Trying to look as pro-fessional as I possibly could, I summoned the locals to stand well back and began unscrewing the base of the device. Removing the base of the bomb, I was confronted with what looked like treacle oozing from it. I scraped a small quantity up, and at a safe distance tried to ignite it. After a few attempts I managed to get the dark brown liquid to ignite and a flame about two feet high shot up in front of me. Realizing that what I had here was an oil bomb, I began thinking it shouldn't prove too much of a problem.

I thought the best thing was to ignite the substance inside the case of the bomb and let it burn itself out. With this in mind I moved the spectators, their numbers increasing by the minute, back still further, placed a grenade on top of the device, removed the pin and retired immediately to the 'safety' of a nearby bush. Crouched behind the bush Marine Turfrey and I waited for the explosion. Once the dust had settled, we could see that the bomb still remained intact. My next reckoning was to set light to it, so gathering as much wood as we could find we built a bonfire around the cursed thing. The dry brushwood readily burst into flame, and my mate and I hid behind our bush once more. The flames became fiercer and soon they were licking inside the base of the bomb. Suddenly, there was a mighty roar and a flame some 100 feet high leapt skywards, simultaneously, our refuge, the bush, ignited from the intense heat. Miraculously we escaped with no more than singed eyelashes. It was bloody hot though! The fire soon died down and eventually extinguished itself. The show now over, the villagers returned to their houses.

Naturally we were the toast of the village, and just as naturally we had to be toasted. The night left me with two heads, and I don't know what house or to whom it belonged that I slept in that night. Come morning, I lifted myself from the concrete floor, poured cold water over my head and made ready to leave.

As soon as we had landed on the island with our prisoners the locals had offered to lock them up in their nick for us, which was a great help. The time had now come to collect them. Safely back on the caique once more, all that was left was to wave farewell to our grateful hosts and set sail for Chios.

The journey back to base was relatively pleasant. There was a slight swell on the water which made the cruise more interesting, for us that is. The Italians were not such good sailors and were convinced that they would drown. Apart from being seasick, they spent much of the voyage in prayer. The Greek crew cooked a meal which I thoroughly enjoyed, that is until I found out it was octopus, then I wanted to be sick! I could feel the excitement rising in me as Chios came into sight, after all I was anxious to show off the general I had captured.

We entered the harbour and came alongside the jetty where quite a crowd had gathered to greet us. It transpired that, as we had not been heard of since our boat had sunk, we were considered lost at sea. My CO was waiting on the jetty, and as I stepped from the boat he greeted me warmly, asking how everything had gone. Sticking out my chest with pride, I responded that I had in fact captured an Italian general. The major looked me up and down, with a look that suggested he was wondering whether I had been on too many raids, or been suffering the effects of too much sun, or even too much of the local hooch? As the prisoners disembarked from the caique and were duly led away, I presented the general to my CO. He looked him over, and then went into hysterics. 'General, he's not a bloody general Bill, he's a sergeant major.' he chortled. I was as sick as a parrot. To think I had lavished such care and attention on this elaborately, suited and booted apology for a soldier. I thought, right, he would pay for this, but how? 'The boots. That's it, I'll take his bloody boots.' Luckily the riding boots fitted me, so I found the Italian a pair of Army boots, pimples and all, and did a swap. When I resumed my duties as a police patrolman, I was the envy of all my mates, telling them that my prisoner had presented me with the boots. Hadn't he? Marine Turfrey, my number two during the recent escapades, had really won his spurs. I had found him eager, reliable, and cool in emergencies. In future I would have no reservations whatsoever about embarking on raids with him.

With the Germans long departed, Chios had become the base for our navy. The harbour was now cluttered with submarines, gunboats and the latest torpedo boats. Most of the time the job of policing the island was boring, although at times Jolly Jack Tar livened things up a bit with runs ashore. Boredom began to set in and we pondered what might be in store for us marines. With most of the islands now liberated, the few that were still occupied by the enemy were left very much to their own devices, with little or no help likely to come from their fatherland. The war was coming to an end.

We were getting ready for evening patrol, thinking that perhaps we had seen the last of any action, when we were summoned to prepare to leave the island. Our detachment of ten marines, all that were on the island, hastily gathered equipment and weapons in readiness for orders. We were told to proceed to the jetty and board a caique that was waiting in readiness for us. With renewed excitement at what might be afoot, we approached the harbour to find a real hive of activity. Every caique available was being loaded with men from the Sacred Squadron and their gear. It was obviously something big and we were more than eager to find out what.

Once aboard our allotted craft our curiosity was soon satisfied. We were informed that the purpose of the raiding force now gathering, was to facilitate the liberation of the island of Milos; this island was a German stronghold, and heavily defended. Our intelligence bods had discovered that the enemy garrison on Milos consisted of 600 Germans, backed up with a whole range of heavy weapons, including batteries of the dreaded 88mm guns. To hamper and discourage any attempted assault, the garrison was encased behind walls of reinforced concrete, six feet thick.

With just forty-five Greeks and ten marines, one wondered just how it was expected that we could dislodge the enemy from their stronghold. Then we received further intelligence along the lines of, 'The enemy is disenchanted and morale is at an all time low. They will surrender to a show of force.' I thought, 'I've heard that one before somewhere.' Our raiding force headed out to sea and as dawn was approaching we closed on the island of Milos.

We knew the Germans had an outpost on the island ready to signal uninvited visitors, so decided to take it out. Our small armada hove to, and soldiers of the Sacred Squadron landed, closely followed by us marines. As we hit the beach, more-or-less together, out of nowhere came a number of donkeys with handlers in readiness to load our gear onto the animal's backs and follow us wherever we might go.

With a Greek scout in the lead, moving quietly, we approached the enemy outpost. Suddenly the scout halted, and motioned us to lie low. We dived for the cover of the hedgerow, from where we observed a sentry with his rifle slung over his shoulder pacing up and down. The Greek scout had vanished into the darkness. The sentry came to the end of his beat, then turned to retrace his steps. The unfortunate soldier was not to know that it would be the last movement he would ever make. From his hiding place, and as silently as a shadow, the scout pounced on the sentry. There was no noise, and in an instant the Greek was lowering the sentry to the ground and dragging him into the undergrowth.

Now unobserved, we were able to take up our positions on a small hill overlooking the outpost. As dawn approached we set up our weapons ready to attack.

There would be no dialogue with the enemy. They would have to be silenced as quickly as possible, although it might be difficult to do this before they had the chance to make contact with their main garrison. As daylight broke we could see the enemy clearly and our trigger fingers tightened as we waited for the command to open fire.

The order to open fire was rapped out like a rifle shot. Sighting my Bren gun, I squeezed the trigger. The sudden burst of fire caused the Germans to panic and run around like headless chickens. A soldier ran across my line of fire and keeping him in my sights I squeezed off a five-second burst; the curved arc of the tracer caught him and he fell to the ground. The British Army .303 Bren gun was a fantastic weapon. Just a handful of men have been known to keep a considerable number of the enemy pinned down with these guns. They were deadly accurate, and would kill an enemy stone dead at distances of up to a mile. When they were set up effectively, the crossfire left you nowhere to run.

Unlike some other raids we did not hoist a white flag suggesting we wanted to talk, this time we rose as one man and charged the enemy, firing our weapons as we ran. Firing a Bren from the hip is strenuous, but effective. There is relatively little recoil. On the contrary, a Bren gun tends to pull away from you. A number of commando lads used these weapons in this fashion, on a regular basis. The surprise had been complete and we were among them before they could gather their senses.

Expecting this to be quite a big show, we had with us an American correspondent, who fortunately spoke fluent German. Just how fortunate this was we were soon to discover. Charging into the enemy communications room, I was stopped in my tracks by a telephone ringing madly. I seized the instrument and put it to my ear – unsurprisingly the German tongue that greeted my eardrum sounded alarmed. Understanding not a word of German, I passed the receiver to the American who was close at hand. The Yank had been briefed in readiness for such an incident and asked to speak to the garrison commander, who came on the phone, and thinking he was talking to one of his own men asked what all the shooting was about. You can imagine his surprise when the American identified himself, and informed him that a British force had landed, and in order to avoid any unnecessary bloodshed the German officer should surrender his forces to us.

The garrison commander blew his top and told the correspondent in no uncertain terms just where to stick the British force, and that if we wanted his troops then we had better come and try to get them. This was not the news we wanted, although with 600 men under his command we didn't really expect him to surrender without a fight.

From an adjacent room I could hear a lot of arguing and decided to see what it was all about. On entering the room the sight of a Greek sergeant arguing with a German soldier confronted me.

When I enquired what all the fuss was about, the German, who spoke quite good English, explained that he was a medical orderly and that the Greek had taken his first aid bag, which the medic now needed urgently. I held the rank of corporal, so wondered what the sergeant's reaction would be if I ordered him to return the bag. My request was met with a stern rebuff. I persisted with my order, 'Give the medic his bag, now.' The atmosphere, already tense, hotted up. The sergeant threatened me – so I threatened him.

Things were going from bad to worse. The Greek sergeant reached down and put his hand on his revolver. In no mood to back down I reached for mine. There we stood, face to face, like a scene from a John Wayne movie. My heart pounded. I hoped I could out-draw the Greek but I had made up my mind not to hesitate, if he moved to draw his gun, I would draw and fire simultaneously. I wasn't going to give this awkward cuss a chance to shoot me. Then to my great relief, without further argument, the sergeant threw the first aid bag at the German medic and walked away.

The Greeks, especially the Sacred Squadron, were fearless fighters, but they could also be loose cannons. Volatile, you could never be sure how they would react. Their lands had been under the jackboot; they and their families had suffered much hardship and acts of violence from their oppressors. I suppose they could be forgiven for wanting, at every opportunity, to seek revenge.

The enemy were on a hill, with the valley stretched out in front of them. We positioned ourselves at the opposite end, from where we could observe every movement of the garrison. They in turn could survey us through their field glasses. Thankfully, the Germans had no idea of our strength (or they might have laughed). Our wireless operator was picking up the enemy signals and replaying them to us. He received a signal, which had been sent by the garrison informing its headquarters that it was under attack and requesting assistance. The reply from their HQ was that assistance was impossible and that they must fight to the last man. The enemy's garrison commander replied 'We will. Out.' The answer from his HQ came back in one word. 'Goodbye.'

We were now virtually at stalemate, and could only sit and watch for enemy movements and once in a while give the odd burst of gunfire just to let them know we were still out there. Likewise, the enemy returned our fire, but without effect.

Three days of cat and mouse had passed when a decision was

made to enlist the help of the Royal Navy, who were now a force to be reckoned with in the Aegean. The navy offered to send a light cruiser to bombard the enemy gun positions. The cruiser duly arrived, and from it came a spotter, who would plot the fall of fire. Three marines escorted the Navy spotter to the best possible vantage point, staying to protect him should the enemy send a patrol out.

The spotter radioed the positions back to the cruiser and we waited for the reaction. It came in seconds. A deafening crash. The big guns on the cruiser had spoken. The whine of shells in the first salvo whistled above our heads. I thought, 'I'm bloody glad I'm not on the receiving end.' We eagerly watched the result. The first salvo scored a bullseye, with the shells landing spot on target. When the smoke and dust cleared, instead of the gaping hole in the enemy's defences we expected, to our disappointment the position targeted remained virtually unscathed. The second salvo did little more than the first. More disappointment came when the navy spotter said that to order another salvo would be pointless. He said it was obvious that the guns on the cruiser were too light to cause any serious damage to the enemy's defences, and added it would take something much heavier to breach the position.

The enemy decided it was his turn to retaliate and for the first time we heard his big guns bark. Fearsome they may have sounded, but the shells failed to land anywhere near the cruiser as she turned about and put to sea.

We returned to the status quo, with each side watching the other. Occasionally, possibly to relieve the monotony, the enemy fired their big guns at our positions. Since we had taken refuge in a huge cave we were reasonably safe from any gunfire. Realizing the comparative safety of our position, some of the villagers moved in with us, bringing their goats and donkeys with them! The smell was far from exotic.

We marines were given the task of patrolling the front line, reporting any enemy activity back to base. Now would not be a good time for the Germans to come out after us. We were only ten in number. We increased our bouts of random fire on the enemy positions, hoping to discourage any thoughts they might have of sending out a reconnaissance patrol, and so discovering our ruse.

We waited and waited, then an airstrike was called for and once again we had a grandstand view of the attack. Sadly, like the shells from the cruiser, the bombs dropped by the RAF were not sufficiently heavy to do any serious damage. We decided that the stalemate had gone on long enough and thought it was time for some kind of direct action. We marines were detailed to approach the enemy position under the cover of darkness and open up with our Bren guns, drawing the enemy's fire, whilst, we were told, the Sacred Squadron would storm the garrison.

We waited for darkness to fall and when it did, together with my colleagues we advanced towards the enemy lines. Creeping along a goat track, we got close enough to observe the German sentries patrolling. Without a murmur, we lay on our stomachs and sighted our weapons on the enemy. The officer with us, a major, gave the command to fire, and as he did so five Bren guns barked, raking the enemy positions. Then, our ammunition expended, we began to make our withdrawal.

Whilst we were firing, at first, the enemy did not retaliate; instead they waited until we had stopped. This was typical German strategy, making you fire first before attempting to return fire – no fools. Now we got a dose of small arms fire, and this, together with the mortar shells they lobbed at us, made life pretty uncomfortable as we crawled back along the goat track.

Daring to take my eyes off the man in front, I glanced upwards and was amazed at just how close the barrage of fire was. The enemy fire was so accurate, tracer bullets were screaming literally inches above our heads. If we hadn't been crawling on our stomachs we would have been killed. Mortar shells were still exploding all around us; the enemy was trying to anticipate our progress and aiming in front of us. Thankfully they were misjudging the range. I was wondering just how long it would be before they got it right when all fell silent. It was nerve-racking. We listened for the sound of gunfire coming from our Greek friends as they attacked, but none came.

Still not daring to stand upright, we eventually reached the end of the goat track and comparative safety. We were now out of the range of small arms fire, but there was still no sound to be heard from our troops. The silence was eerie. Had we pulled out too soon? It was too late to return now. A little more than weary and thankful that we hadn't suffered any casualties, we made our way back to our cave HQ, still wondering what had happened to the Sacred Squadron.

Back in the sanctuary of our cave, there was another crisis. A young girl who was taking refuge with us, was screaming with pain. She was about to give birth. A naval doctor was summoned from one of the cruisers, and with a little assistance from the new mother's friends, a baby girl was delivered. Amid smiles and cheers from the girl's parents, we were all declared honorary uncles. On a war torn island, whose people had suffered loss of life and destruction, a new life, a tiny hope for the future. Nature never ceases to amaze – life goes on.

The following morning a naval cutter put ashore, and the captain of the cruiser stepped out. We greeted him and escorted him to our cave. When we reported the previous night's action to him, and enquired about the expected assistance from the Greeks, he looked startled. He asked, 'Didn't you receive a signal saying the Sacred Squadron had been called away to liberate another island?' We assured him we had received no such message.

Since our fighting force on the island now consisted of ten marines plus one officer, we were concerned about our fate if the enemy garrison decided to come out and have a go. The naval captain was just as concerned and advised that we be evacuated as soon as possible. Although this went very much against the grain, as no marine likes walking away from a fight, it certainly made good sense. Arrangements were being made to lift us off the island the following morning. As dawn broke two cutters from a Navy destroyer at anchor in the bay, were seen approaching the beach. Hastily we collected together our equipment and weapons and with a sigh of relief the last man boarded a cutter. Soon we were making for the destroyer.

It so happened that our evacuation hadn't come too soon. Looking back at the island we could see the enemy's vehicles probing out from their positions. They must have come to the conclusion that we obviously hadn't much of a force, or by now we would have stormed them. It looked as though they were going to chance their arm and come looking for us. Sorry to disappoint you Adolf, but much as we bootnecks love a fight, we also have a brain, and know exactly when to bugger off! Although we had not been able to liberate Milos this time, we knew the enemy's days were numbered. They would soon be mopped up.

We boarded the destroyer and settled in. Soon the ship weighed anchor and began making way for Alexandria. We knew that this was pretty well the end of hostilities in the Aegean and thought that we would soon return to Blighty to retrain for the conflict in the Far East.

We had a very welcome break in Alexandria; a run ashore for a few beers, and a much needed haircut. We spent a few days in that fascinating city before boarding a troopship bound for England. Dear old England – she was never so inviting as she was now.

After a spot of leave, during which I took the long awaited chance to visit once again my family and friends, I returned to my unit. Back at camp once more I found that training had already begun in earnest for the Far East. However, before our training was completed, the war in Europe was over and with the dropping of the atomic bomb, which forced Japan to surrender, the Second World War finally came to an end. Hopefully, the next stop would be Civvy Street and I can't say that I felt sorry. I would miss my comrades, that was for sure, but like so many others, I was weary of war, and was glad for the sake of everyone that it was all over.

Chapter 9

Policeman in Malaya

I applied and was accepted to attend an interview, to become a conductor on a London trolleybus. At the time, London Transport rules determined that, if you wanted to drive one of their vehicles, you had first to serve an apprenticeship of two years as a conductor. I had to start somewhere, and this seemed as good a way to re-habilitate myself as any. I was offered a job, which I promptly accepted, then sat and passed the statutory entrance exam.

I rather enjoyed conducting a trolleybus through the streets of London. Dealing with passengers those days was very easy. Having withstood the strains of the Blitz on London, most folk were grateful to have come through it all and very rarely complained about anything. I considered my best passengers to be the early morning cleaning ladies on their way to clean shops and offices. They were the salt of the earth, always cheerful and ready with a quip or two.

One incident involving the early morning cleaning brigade will always stand out in my memory. I had picked up my usual ladies at 5.00 a.m. A few stops further on a trio of villainous looking characters tried to board my bus without paying any fare. They said they had been out all night gambling and lost every penny they had. The largest of the trio stepped onto the platform saying that he and his mates were going to ride on the bus and just what did I think I could do about it? I had guessed they were trouble as soon as I clapped eyes on them. But before I could make any move or do anything a voice from behind me chirped up, 'No money – no ride'. Then like a magician's wand, an umbrella appeared and cracked the big fellow over the head. With a look of sheer amazement on his face and rubbing a sore head, he staggered from the platform back into the gutter. Any thoughts the villains might have had of retaliation were soon dispelled when they saw my leading lady, now reinforced by her colleagues, all suitably armed and ready for action. The bus pulled away to the chuckles of my ladies, who have my eternal gratitude. If Hitler's troops had landed on England's soil they would have had to face these magnificent women. The prospect of that is best left to the imagination. I, for one, would sooner face the Germans!

There turned out to be a shortage of drivers, so I didn't have to wait for the statutory period to elapse before being eligible to apply for a driving job. I passed the driving course and test as laid down by London Transport, and was now a fully-fledged trolleybus driver. Working on the buses seemed to be a different world and for a time I was content, but before long my old feet started to itch and the feeling of unrest and wanderlust spread.

The conflict in Korea erupted so, not wanting to miss out on any action that might be on offer, I hastily made my way to the nearest recruiting office to volunteer my services. They couldn't possibly manage without me, could they? It seems they thought they could, for they told me that as I was still on Z reserve from the last conflict, I would have to wait for call up. That is, they added, if in fact the Z reservists would be called upon at all.

Dolefully I returned to my driving job, and waited patiently for the postman every morning; but I waited in vain. It became increasingly clear to me that the Ministry of Defence thought it could manage quite all right without ex-Corporal Bill Sparks DSM RM.

The months dragged by and the feeling of unrest was just as bad. Then once more Lady Luck smiled upon me, only now in the guise of the emergency in Malaya, though this time I was not in any hurry to report to the recruitment centre, the military had had their chance. Instead, I replied to an advertisement that had been placed in the newspapers by the Federation of Malaya Police Force for candidates for posts as police lieutenants. The advert stated that you needed to be 'suitably qualified'. I was confident I could satisfy them that I was.

You can imagine my feeling of enjoyment when I received notice to appear before a selection committee. My interview was successful, now all I had to do was return to my driving job with London Transport and wait for further orders. Finally the day I had been longing for came. On the mat lay an official looking buff coloured envelope, which I opened in haste. I was not disappointed. Inside was a list of instructions, together with an air ticket to Singapore. I was walking on air.

Excitedly, as I boarded the plane at Heathrow, I thought, 'At last I am back in harness.' Although the job on the buses had had its moments, after five years in the marines it was a trifle tame. I had found it almost impossible to settle. The aircraft I was now sitting in was an old four-engine Argonaut and as we taxied to the runway, I reflected on the various old kites I had already entrusted with my life, and thought, one more wouldn't hurt! The pilot pushed back the throttles and we raced along the runway, then lifted into the night sky. I could see the lights of old London twinkling below; I had longed to be reunited with my home town, and now felt ungrateful at leaving her so soon.

The journey should have taken three days, with stops at Rome, Cairo, Bahrain, Karachi, Bombay and Singapore. It was morning when we landed in Rome and we were allowed off the plane for a few minutes to stretch our legs. After a short spell we took off for Cairo and thence to Bahrain, landing there that evening. After taking on fuel we left Bahrain and, as we circled the city, I looked down at the myriad of lights forming dizzy patterns in the blackness – like stars. Soon I was nodding off on my own Milky Way. I must have been asleep for about an hour before I woke up and looked out of the window. I could not believe my eyes, surely the lights I was looking down on were the very same as those I had seen as we left Bahrain. Convincing myself that, during the hours of darkness, most cities look much the same from the air, I settled.

We began to circle and I looked out of the window again when, to my horror, I noticed that one propeller was not turning. I couldn't help thinking, 'After all the scrapes I've been in, surely it's not going to end like this?' Then through a crackling intercom came a voice. 'This is your captain speaking. You may have noticed that we have trouble with one of our engines. There is absolutely no cause for alarm – I can fly this plane on the remaining three engines that are still running smoothly. We have returned to Bahrain to effect the necessary repair, and will be landing soon.'

No need for alarm! I love these guys. You are a couple of miles up, one engine has failed and you are praying the other three are not going to follow suit, and they tell you there is no cause to alarm yourself! I braced myself as the landing lights came up to greet us.

Then, with only the very slightest of bumps, the plane was down and racing along the runway. The captain had been true to his word; he could fly the aircraft perfectly with only three engines.

I looked out of the window as we slowed on the runway and could see ambulances and fire engines racing close by. When the plane finally came to a halt, I climbed down the steps onto mother earth with a feeling of relief and gratitude. All of the passengers were taken to a departure lounge and offered coffee. Thanks!

Repairs to the aircraft were effected and before long we were boarding the plane once more to continue the next leg of our journey. The aircraft flew smoothly and we landed in Karachi the following morning, just in time for breakfast. Refreshed and the plane re-fuelled we boarded once more. With a feeling of elation and a spring in my steps, and in the knowledge that we were getting nearer to Singapore, I bounded up the steps of the old aeroplane.

The plane taxied to the runway and turned into the wind ready for take off. As the engines raced I braced myself in anticipation of the lurch I expected as we hurtled along the tarmac. The lurch never came. Instead, with the engines throttled back, the pilot taxied the plane back to the airport buildings. Once more we disembarked and were led to a departure lounge, (more coffee) where we were told to wait whilst our plane received attention. It transpired that another engine had failed and, had the pilot tried to get the plane airborne, it would have been curtains for us all. I was rapidly losing my sense of humour with this old kite.

This time we were delayed by twenty-four hours whilst mechanics changed the faulty engine. However unsettling this was, it did give us a chance to see do a little sightseeing. The following morning, without incident, we took off for Bombay. Needless to say, I kept an ever-watchful eye on the engines, not that I could have done anything had one failed. Thankfully, all went well and we reached our destination without further mishap. The journey onward to our final destination, Singapore, was also uneventful. And so it was with a sigh and a feeling of relief, when the plane came to a halt that I walked down the steps and onto the tarmac, knowing I would remain on the ground for a while at least.

Waiting to meet our plane was a lieutenant from the Malayan Police Force, and it was very much to my surprise, when I saw a clip-board in his hand on which other names were written as well as mine. It transpired that three of my fellow passengers were also would-be police officers. One would have thought that with all the goings-on during the long flight, we might have stumbled on one another. Now, of course, we recognized each other as fellow travellers, and had a bloody good laugh about it. However, the laughter soon came to an end when the lieutenant answered our numerous questions and briefed us. To be honest, he did not paint too rosy a picture of what lay ahead.

He had indicated, and in the coming days this was to be substantiated, that the higher echelon were not too eager to confront the present emergency. Many of the police chiefs had been in their jobs prior to the hostilities and enjoyed a very nice way of life. They were in no mood to fight anyone. When the trouble first began, they were like fish out of water and relied on the lieutenants to take the brunt of the action, while at the same time treating them with a degree of disdain. This was not the best of introductions to my new job, but I was determined not to pre-judge the situation; I would wait and see for myself.

The police officer drove us to his headquarters, which was situated in a naval barracks. There we were issued with our warrant cards and kitted out. Our uniform consisted of a couple of khaki drill shirts, trousers, a blue beret, a peaked cap, a set of jungle greens and a pair of jungle boots. A bit sparse, I thought, when considering what I had been used to in the marines. No training was given for the job in hand and, as with our contemporaries, we new officers would have to rely on our own initiative and woe betide us if we got it wrong. We were advised that we could expect no support from our superiors; on the contrary they would take any opportunity to discredit us.

The situation was delicate and complex politically. The main product of the country was rubber. All the plantation managers were Europeans, most of them British. Unfortunately, some were suspect, by virtue of the fact that the only thing they were concerned about was getting their rubber out. It was a common belief among the lieutenants, but not proven, that some were even paying the bandits not to attack, or cause any trouble, on their plantations.

The senior police officers went to great lengths not to displease the Malayan politicians, and so refrained from pressing any advice or suggestions, that they deemed to be unpopular amongst the Malays. So this was the general picture of things. I would have to bear it all in mind as I went about my duties. We had been in Singapore for only three or four days before we were dispersed to the various states allotted.

Another lieutenant and myself were dispatched to the town of Seremban in the state of Negri Sembilan. Travelling there by rail we spent many uncomfortable hours, always aware that the train might come under attack from bandits, be derailed, or suffer a breakdown; all three were common occurrences at the time. At some length and with nerves jingling we arrived at Seremban, where we were met by another officer who informed us that since there was no room available at the officers' mess he would take us to a government resthouse. Our stay there was short. The next morning we were collected and conveyed to the police station, where we met the officer supervising police manpower. He delegated an area for us to police.

The supervising officer appeared extremely well informed and told me that in view of my war record he had the perfect assignment for me, the village of Ayer Hitam – the site of a small plantation some fifty miles into the jungle where bandit activity was strong. I would have to watch my step. Access to my destination was by armoured train, which ran just once daily. There was a road, but this was definitely out of bounds to us – the bandits had control of it.

An English planter, who lived there with his wife and one child, managed the plantation. His assistant was also English. The population of the village was around 200, made up mostly of Malays, Chinese and Tamils. The Chinese and the Tamils were employed as tappers whilst the Malays mooched around in their own laid back (lazy) style.

I was taken to the small town of Bahau, from where I was to catch the train to the plantation. Before boarding, I visited the armoury where I drew a .38 pistol and an American carbine – a quick firing rifle, but not much stopping power. I made ready to leave and hoped my journey would proceed without any interruption from bandits.

I boarded my train. Literally, it was now *my* train. Once it had left Bahau, I was responsible for it. Thankfully, without incident, the train lurched and swayed for about half an hour until we reached Ayer Hitam where, on alighting, I was met by the lieutenant I had come to relieve. He greeted me warmly and made no bones about how pleased he was to see me. This caused me to wonder just what I had let myself in for.

The police station was adjacent to the railway track, isolated, but a fortress. I judged that if we came under attack, always providing I could rely on my fellow officers, the position could be easily defended. Introducing myself, I inspected my police force who were almost all special constables and mainly Malay. I admit to being a tad disappointed with those standing before me. They looked, all in all, a poor lot, so I didn't expect too much from them. I would have to train them in my own way, but as they were operational this could only be done between duties and with their co-operation. Their uniforms were in tatters and when I inquired from my predecessor why they weren't properly clothed, he told me that, try as he might, although new issues of clothing had been promised, nothing ever materialized. I was determined to do better.

I was escorted along a dirt track road that led to the village; the only passage. Wooden shacks lined the road – the dwelling places of the locals. One large shack served as the village shop, where local men congregated to pass the time with friends and often engage, behind closed doors, in a spot of gambling. Although gambling was illegal, for the most part we turned a blind eye, but made a token raid once in a while just to let them know we were aware of the activity.

My predecessor wasted no time introducing me to the plantation manager and his assistant. I was not impressed. Then, after a couple more days spent showing me around, he took his leave wishing me the very best of luck. From what I had seen so far, I was bloody well going to need it! However, there was one feature of the estate that did impress me, and that was the group of Gurkhas stationed there. The sight of these lovely blokes did wonders for my confidence.

My first action was to get my troops on parade, where I could put them through some basic drill to see what they knew. They were an undisciplined rabble and it was immediately obvious that a great deal of work was needed to get them anywhere near a standard where they could be relied on. My next step was to see what kind of marksmen they were. I was pleasantly surprised by the performance of some – they were quite good shots. Just how good they would be should they come under fire from the bandits, at this stage, was left to the imagination. It is a different kettle of fish altogether to keep your nerve and take aim calmly when bullets are raining down on you. Only time would tell.

My police station was about five miles from the estate and that was where the Gurkhas were billeted so, should we come under attack it would be some time before the Nepalese soldiers could come to our assistance. The only method of communication between us was a field telephone, which could be sabotaged quite easily. I decided to put things to the test and came up with an exercise without informing my policemen, except that is for one sergeant who was the only regular officer on the station. I had already drilled my men on what action should be taken if we came under fire, and supposing that our lines of communication were broken. I had instructed them that after taking up their positions, a stream of tracer bullets would be fired into the air as a warning to the Gurkha sentry that we were under attack. Hopefully the sentry would spot the tracer and raise the alarm.

One evening, at the first opportunity my sergeant sounded the alarm. And whilst the policemen ran immediately to their allotted posts, it was amid confusion. Some forgot to take their rifles and others argued as to who should be where. I fired a Bren gun into the air, but there was no response. We were obviously too far away for the Gurkha sentry to see the tracer from the gun. It was all a bit of a shambles, but I did learn something from it. My policemen would need a lot of drill and instruction to cope with any emergency – a bit of a daunting task. I was also extremely unhappy about not being able to attract the attention of the Gurkhas – should our phone line get cut.

Each day we rose at the crack of dawn and set up a roadblock in order to search all the tappers before they left the village in order to prevent them from taking food out to the bandits. It was a known fact that some bandits infiltrated the village, to intimidate the tappers into bringing them food, cigarettes and money. One poor Chinese girl, who had resisted, was found with her throat cut.

It soon became obvious that the bandits in this region had been allowed to come and go pretty much at will terrifying the locals into serving their every whim. Nobody had tried to stop this. In fact, they were, through intimidation, forced to work against the authorities. Those who were in sympathy with the movement warned the bandits in advance of any likely danger. It was dangerous to trust any of the natives.

One day, I was standing under the shade of a tree, to keep away from the blistering heat while watching my policemen execute a routine roadblock, when from the corner of my eye I was aware of a shadow waving around immediately behind me. I thought it was being caused by the large leaves on the tree under which I sheltered. Suddenly, my lady police officer let out a mighty scream and pointed. On turning my head I found I was looking straight into the eyes of a giant king cobra; he was about to settle on my shoulder. Snakes move quickly, but not as quickly as I did! In a flash, I ducked away, and as the thing opened its hood, I managed to fire two shots through its head. Although the incident aged me ten years in as many seconds, at least it proved my reflexes were in fine fettle – even if I did need a change of underpants!

One night I received information that bandits were coming into the *kampong*. I was determined that they would come to realize they could not carry on just as they pleased whilst I was in charge, so I organized an ambush. I selected the ones who I thought were my six best men and led them to the path I had been shown the bandits were likely to enter by. Carefully, I placed my troops. I say carefully, as in the past it had been known for them to shoot at each other whilst trying to ambush the enemy.

I chose a position, then lying down, waited for my first kill. Apart from the now familiar jungle noises, at first all was deathly quiet, then suddenly voices. My pulse quickened as I strained my eyes through the darkness for movement. I listened. I could still hear voices, but they did not appear to get any nearer. Then it dawned on me that it was not the enemy who was doing the talking; it was my own bloody men. Down at the bottom of the line two of my policemen were having a chat as if they were in a bar somewhere. It was futile to continue the surveillance with any hope of an ambush, since the voices could have been heard far away. Any bandits who might have been in the vicinity would be long gone by now.

I marched my squad back to the station, where I gave them the mother and father of all bollockings. It was pointless trying to do anything else about it, my 'specials' were not cut out to be fighters. Frustrated to say the very least, I continued with my policing duties as best I could, given the quality, or lack of it, of my troops. I guess it must have been a similar situation on every estate that relied largely on special constables.

The *kampong* drew its water from a pumping station situated outside the perimeter wire, further into the jungle. Each morning the water pump operator had to be escorted by police to the pumping station. At that early morning hour, anyone found outside the wire was officially deemed hostile. One day, much to the surprise of the escort, I decided to accompany them. I wondered why they seemed uneasy at my presence; I was soon to find out.

As we left the *kampong* and approached the jungle fringe, three men emerged into a clearing. 'Bandits' thought I and opened fire. The bandits scattered whilst my police constables looked on in horror. Apparently this was quite a regular encounter but previously my men had been too frightened to engage them. I was devastated. Just what would it take to make decent policemen out of these people? I threatened to charge them with cowardice, but thought that futile, as it would get no backing from my superiors. The days wore on and I was still yet to make a kill, and with the crowd I had under me I wasn't likely to. I had to do something, or go mad with frustration.

I paid a visit to the Gurkha camp and, during a conversation with the British officer in charge, discovered that he was about to send a patrol into the jungle. I asked to accompany the Gurkha patrol, not as an officer, but as one of the men. The officer looked quite surprised but readily agreed, providing that I took my orders from the patrol leader and didn't try to interfere in any way. I was overjoyed, at last a chance of action with some real troops.

The following morning, well before daylight, I met up with the Gurkha patrol. In single file, behind the troop commander, we moved off into the jungle. I was confident that, if we met up with any bandits, they would get short shrift. I admit the patrol was tough; these little men moved through the jungle with ease and could read every sign it offered but it was a privilege and an education to be with them. I learned a lot.

When the patrol was over, I reluctantly said farewell to my Nepalese friends and returned to my police station. Now I was even more disappointed with my troops than before, but had to make the best of it. I continued with the routine duties; they were all my bunch was capable of and at even these menial tasks they weren't brilliant.

I was supervising a routine roadblock search one morning when one of my policemen discovered a quantity of olive oil. This was something that could be very useful to the bandits for a number of reasons, but instead of quietly noting which container it came from, he danced about as though he had won the national lottery. I was furious with him. We could have followed the lorry discreetly and caught the culprit when he tried to liberate the oil. Still, I didn't give up all hope of nicking a bandit or two and, concealing myself in the cab of the lorry, spent the rest of the day travelling around the estate waiting for someone to chance their luck. It might have been fruitless, but it let everyone know we were alert.

A few days later it was decided to send a night train to the capital, Kuala Lumpur. Pretty vulnerable, when under the cover of darkness, this night train rarely ran for fear of being attacked by bandits. Although there might have been a very good reason for sending this one, I never discovered it. Dawn broke to the shrill of the telephone bell ringing in my ear. As I picked up the receiver I thought this can only mean trouble. An excited voice at the other end of the phone informed me that my train had been derailed and that I was required to escort a repair party to the scene.

This was no job for my constables, so I phoned the Gurkhas and requested that they send a squad to accompany me. They agreed without hesitation and in no time a squad of smiling Nepalese soldiers arrived at my station. We boarded the breakdown rail truck and shot off to rescue the stricken train. I fully expected to find a welcoming party of bandits waiting, as was their custom, but there was none. I can only put this down to the presence of the Gurkhas. Had I had my constables with me, I am sure I would have been in for a fight. Very few fancy an altercation with Gurkha troops, they are as fearsome in action as their history suggests.

It took all day for engineers to repair the line and place the train back on the track. Tired out, from the constant state of alertness, I was thankful when the job was at an end and I was back in my station.

I never dreamed I would get bored with this job, but I was at a loss to find anything meaningful with which to occupy my time. If I had had a decent squad of men around me, I feel sure I could have made myself busier. Suddenly, and completely out of the blue, I received information that bandits were planning to infiltrate the village again.

Determined there would not be a repeat of the last fiasco, I put

my men through some rigorous drill without a mention of the likelihood of action, until I was reasonably satisfied with their
performance. Now I threatened them with a fate worse than death
should they let me down. Casually, I made a reconnaissance of the
perimeter fence and discovered a place where the wire had been cut.
Instead of ordering a repair to the fence immediately, as normally
I would have done, I walked past as though I had not noticed
anything untoward. I now had a good idea of the bandits' possible
point of entry.

Soon after dark I marched my men into the compound. A curfew
was in force so we were able to move unobserved. I placed my men
in the most advantageous positions, then, lying down myself, I
waited. Suddenly a huge flame lit the darkened sky. It came from
a bonfire outside a Tamil hut. I thought, 'Sod it. It has obviously
been lit to warn the bandits of a pending ambush.' I was furious
and determined to arrest the man responsible and approached the
wooden hut he had been seen to run into.

The door to the hut was locked, so I banged loudly on it,
announcing myself as a police officer and that he had better open
up or I would smash the door down. The culprit shouted something
from behind the door and my Malay driver, who was acting as an
interpreter, informed me that the man had told us to go away. I
repeated my demand adding that unless the door was opened in
five seconds I would break it down. The door flew open and a man
with a knife in one hand tried to rush past me. Instinct took over
and I floored him with a blow to the jaw. He was out cold and
bleeding from the mouth.

Instead of picking the fellow up and taking him away to the cells,
I decided that, as he couldn't run anywhere, I would put him on his
bed, leave him until morning and arrest him then. The next
morning on my way to the compound to arrest the quisling, I was
confronted by a large group of tappers, with their manager in the
middle of them. Plantation managers were automatically desig-
nated honorary police inspectors and this man took full advantage
of the rank. We hadn't got on too well when first we met and things
hadn't improved between us. I would have to tread very carefully,
because the manager hobnobbed with the higher-ranking officers,
so things were stacked in his favour from the outset. I was also
suspicious that, although the bungalow in which he lived was
positioned outside the perimeter fence, it had never come under

attack from bandits, or had they ever threatened him. Such notions I thought prudent to keep to myself.

In a furious temper, the estate manager approached blaming me for the strike he now had on his hands, saying it was due to my actions the previous evening. I tried to explain the facts of what had taken place, but he was not in the least interested in my explanation. The only thing that concerned him was getting his men back to work and getting his rubber out. A storming row ensued, which wasn't good in front of the locals. The manager strode away and as he went muttered something about reporting me to the chief of police and getting me shifted. Under my breath I replied, 'That's fine by me'.

On my return to the station, instead of waiting for a call from the chief, I telephoned him, but as I expected the estate manager had got in first and the chief informed me that an investigating officer was on the way. I knew that my case was doomed to failure when I met the officer who had been sent to investigate at the railway station. He told me that, whilst he was on the estate, he would be staying with the manager – in his bungalow. This was a one-horse race – I wasn't even in the starting stalls.

I wasted no time in telling the investigating officer exactly what I thought of the situation and demanded to be withdrawn from the estate. He immediately granted my request and sent for a replacement, who arrived without delay. I was then told to report to the headquarters in Seremban. At HQ I had a blazing row with the officer supervising the region, who said he was moving me to another estate as soon as a suitable one was found. In the meantime I was to double up with another lieutenant and share his bungalow. For the new job I was allocated another car and a police driver. One of the rules in the force was that police lieutenants were not allowed to drive police cars, although they all did. During my first evening on duty my fellow officer said that he had to attend an investigation at a certain army camp, a few miles out of town. As his driver was on leave, could he use mine? I readily agreed until Malik, (I called him Mac) my driver told me that he had been promised that night off. Apparently he had a bit of a domestic problem that wouldn't wait. The poor fellow looked anxious, so I let him go, saying I would drive the car myself. After all I was a professional driver – trained by London Transport!

Everything was going fine and we arrived at the army camp,

where my colleague completed his enquiries. My partner and I were then preparing to leave the camp and return to our residence, but as I climbed into the driver's seat, a sergeant major asked if we could give him and his friends a lift into town. I had no problem with this, saying I was happy to give them a ride. I soon came to realize that the sergeant major was not alone in wanting a favour. He had with him two more sergeant majors and their wives. I hadn't expected to give a lift to five people, but that is what happened. It was cramped to say the least.

The car groaned and creaked under the weight of its occupants, until eventually we reached the outskirts of the town, where I slowed considerably to negotiate a narrow iron bridge. As I eased the vehicle across the bridge a car was approaching with headlights blazing. Despite dipping the headlights of my car furiously, I could not get the on-coming driver to do the same. I was left with no alternative but to pull the car over as close to the side of the bridge as I could, in order to avoid a possible collision. I heard a dull thud and, thinking it was one of the door handles striking one of the iron stanchions on the bridge, I brought the vehicle to a halt to check what damage had been done. I was furious at the other driver for not stopping and made up my mind to ring through to our next checkpoint and have him arrested. As we were now very close to the town, I suggested to my passengers that they alight and walk the rest of the way. They said they were happy enough to do this and climbed out of the car. That is all except one of the sergeant majors who remained in the back seat slumped against the near-side rear door, with the upper part of his body hanging out of the window. He had been skylarking about during the journey, sticking his head out of the window and shouting to everyone we passed. It tran- spired that, as we crossed the bridge, he stuck his head out of the window once too often and was struck by an iron stanchion. That was the dull thud I had heard. I shone my torch through the inky blackness was sickened by the amount of blood splattered over the outside of the car.

Without delay or consultation I jumped back in the car and sped off to the hospital, although I knew in my heart it was futile. A doctor at the hospital confirmed my worst fears – the sergeant major was stone dead.

I 'phoned the duty officer at police headquarters and reported the accident. The officer arrived promptly, accompanied by a breakdown truck, which took my vehicle to the police compound. The following morning I went to the police station and made a full statement and, as expected, was informed there would be an inquiry. I was to be suspended from duty until the outcome was made known. Later the same day I attended the funeral of the unfortunate sergeant major.

The first surprise, and confirmation that I would receive no assistance whatsoever from the higher authorities, came in the form of a summons to attend the local courthouse. I had to answer charges brought against me for an assault on a Tamil rubber tapper – the quisling I had knocked out. I was flabbergasted. I appeared on the due date and, conducting my own defence, argued there was no case to answer.

It soon became all too obvious that the case was cut and dried, I was guilty before I even entered the courthouse. The magistrate had already been instructed and I was fined one hundred dollars – two-thirds of a week's wages. I was furious. All the stories that had been related to me about the hierarchy deserting you in times of trouble were coming true. Somehow, I must have offended one of the cliques, and retribution had been meted out. I was now completely disgruntled with the whole bloody system and determined to do something about it.

My Member of Parliament back home was none other than the old war-horse himself, Winston Churchill. I wrote him a letter reporting on the situation I had found myself in. I didn't receive a reply, but found out, quite by coincidence, that the British Foreign Secretary was not only due to visit Malaya, but Seremban in particular. I was determined to grab the chance to blow the top off the whole bloody affair.

A few days before the Foreign Secretary was due in Seremban I was ordered to report to the Gurkha camp to liaise with them, and since I had grown to love these little brown chaps, I was pleased to have the chance to visit them once more. It was whilst I was away that our Foreign Minister visited Seremban, and he had left before I returned. Convenient for some you might say? Soon I was to be issued with another summons, this time to answer questions about the car accident.

The case dragged on for weeks, until eventually I was found guilty and fined three hundred dollars – two weeks pay. I was rapidly losing my sense of humour. Once again I had no chance;

they were intent on screwing me. I had had enough of these jokers and stormed into the office and told the chief I would refuse all further duties and that he had better send me home. The authorities threatened to stop my pay altogether so I retaliated by saying that, if they did, I would go on a hunger strike. I tried a bluff telling them that I had already alerted the British press of my intentions. It did the trick and they left me to kick my heels in the officers' mess, until one day a few months on I was summoned to the office where I was informed that my contract was to be cancelled and I could go home.

This suited me fine, but it was a disappointment. I had tried so hard to do a professional job in difficult circumstances. Sadly, there were those who, for reasons of vested interest, did not exert themselves to bring the emergency in Malaya to end. They were quite content to sit back and let us lieutenants do the donkey-work and take the flak, whilst they socialized in posh clubs. It was little wonder that bandits could more or less move freely in this country; an advantage which in the end was combated magnificently by British soldiers, many of them were National Servicemen all too many of whom lost their lives. What a waste of good men.

I was overjoyed at the news that I was being sent home by sea, and got on with packing my belongings for the journey. The day came when I finally left Seremban for Singapore – without as much as a glance over my shoulder at the shambles behind me. Three weeks on a pleasure liner, was a wonderful ending to a fruitless and unsavoury twelve months. I had already experienced sufficient character building incidents during my war service and felt I didn't need any more lessons!

The voyage home was most enjoyable. For company I had two other ex-lieutenants who, like me, were glad to be out of it. When we docked at Tilbury it was with mixed feelings that we parted company.

Back home once more I wasted little time before setting out on the job-hunting trail. Employment was scarce but I was prepared to take almost anything and found employment as a labourer on a building site. It was mid-winter and the work very hard. I was given the task of unloading bricks. It was so cold that ice had formed on some and it tore at my hands, so by the end of the day they were raw and bleeding.

The week before Christmas, the foreman informed me that the

job was nearing its end, and that I need not bother coming again. I now had the task of finding something to tide me over until the New Year. All I could find was some casual work as a sorter at the Post Office; another filthy job down in the basement at GPO headquarters. There I received another festive gift – the sack on Christmas Eve – 'Thanks Santa!'

A quiet Christmas passed. I was anxious to find a permanent job but situations were scarce. It was a bad time for the jobless. Eventually, I resorted to my old job of shoe repairing. I had entered the trade after leaving school, but never thought I would return to it. The wages were miserable, but I was desperate and took it in the hope that something better would come along.

My next job was as a milk roundsman. This I enjoyed, that is until the rain came. The damp weather played havoc with my chest and I contracted acute bronchitis. This forced me to change jobs, so I obtained employment as a moulder at a plastics factory. At least I would be working inside and in the warm. Showing an interest in trade union work, I was offered the job as convenor at the works, which I accepted. I enjoyed the challenge of negotiating, but found that, unless I was ever prepared to threaten strike action, the membership were not supportive. This just wasn't my style, and I told my fellow workers so.

Chapter 10

War Crimes Trial

I was getting pretty fed up with life, when one morning, as I was about to leave for work, a buff coloured envelope dropped on the mat. For a while I stood over it looking down. What could it be? It couldn't be my old mob, the SBS, they had already told me I was no longer needed. Slowly, I picked the letter from the mat and carefully slit open the envelope.

Inside, was a communication from the Judge Advocate's office, informing me that I had to attend as a witness at a war crimes Trial to be held in Hamburg, in Germany. The memorandum stated that I was to report to the RTO Liverpool Street station at 19.15 hours on 16 August 1948, ready in all respects to board the Harwich – Hook route (sic) train which departed at 20.00 hours on that date. From the Hook of Holland I was to proceed by train to Hamburg, where I would be met. It was further stated that I would only be allowed to take £5 in sterling out of the country; it was unlikely that I would be able to sample the delights of Hamburg on a fiver!

The trial had been convened to bring justice to those responsible for the barbaric treatment meted out to my mates who had been captured during Operation Frankton. We had seriously damaged six ships, and more seriously, put a mighty dent in Adolf's ego – but at a terrible cost of human life. Two marines had drowned during the passage up the Gironde, and six more men were captured and subsequently executed. Under Hitler's Commando Order, all 'saboteurs' were to be brutally interrogated and then shot forthwith – a blatant breach of the Geneva Convention. Those responsible for murdering my comrades would now be brought to trial.

As the train rumbled through the German countryside, I stared out of the window and was amazed at just how much damage our RAF lads had caused to each town we passed through. They hadn't missed much. London was heavily Blitzed, particularly my East End, but this was something else. I was aware of eyes upon me and tried not to show my self-consciousness. In my new suit and with the temporary rank of captain, I felt somewhat superior as I eagerly awaited my arrival at Hamburg. I had expected to see Colonel Hasler on the train, but so far had not caught sight of him. I thought that he must already be in Hamburg and waiting for me.

As the train steamed to a halt, I stepped onto the platform and made my way out of the station. I then walked the short distance to the Reichoff Hotel where a reservation had been made for me. Two days later, as instructed, I made my way to the building where the war crimes trials were being held, which fortunately was not too far away. As I stood on the pavement opposite the courthouse waiting to cross a busy road, a policeman, who somehow realized that I was British stopped the traffic to let me cross. This courtesy stunned me somewhat. For five years the Germans had been trying to kill me, now one of them was escorting me across the road!

I sat listening intently to the evidence, but it was frustrating hearing all the lies being told by the accused and I could hardly wait to be called upon and given the chance to put the record straight. Colonel Werner von Tippelskirch of Hitler's HQ staff, was in the dock and saying how, when captured, the marines were dressed in plain olive green clothing without any insignia or badges of rank. We were thought to be spies. I stared at von Tippelskirch, and his eagle face stared back at me in defiance. How I would have loved to have walked across the room, placed my hands around his neck and throttled him right there and then. Admiral Bachmann, Commander-in-Chief Western France and Admiral Marschall, Bachmann's superior should also have been in the dock. I've no idea why Marschall was not indicted and Bachmann had been reported as already dead.

Eventually, the prosecuting council called me to the stand, where I answered the questions put to me. I confirmed that during the raid all personnel wore Royal Marine shoulder titles and the distinctive badge of Combined Operations, plus badges of rank where applicable. Now I waited eagerly for the defence counsel to cross-examine me. I was ready for him and determined to give him a hard time. To my surprise and disappointment, he offered no questions and I was told to stand down.

Lieutenant Theodore Prahm, Adjutant of the Naval Officer in charge, Bordeaux, who personally supervised the execution of Wallace and Ewart, was unable to confirm any official order being given to him to carry out the dreadful deed. It was generally accepted that Mick Wallace and Jock Ewart, after interrogation with 'no methods barred' were taken into some woods, tied to stakes and executed. We later discovered that my brave comrades were in fact shot against a wall in a courtyard where they had been imprisoned at the Châteaux Magnol at Blanquefort near Bordeaux. Their bodies were then taken into woods and buried but, despite extensive inquiries, the location of these brave men's graves has never been discovered. Mick and Jock *never* disclosed a thing under interrogation; had they done so the raid would certainly have failed. Without doubt, I owe my life to them. They were 'Mentioned in Dispatches'. They should have been awarded VCs.

The trial dragged on for a couple of months. Eventually von Tippelskirch was acquitted and no one else was ever indicted for this terrible crime. It was with mixed feelings and a heavy heart that I left Germany to return home. I was very disappointed at the outcome. The words spoken by Judge-Advocate Mr C.L. Stirling KC, to Prahm, accusing him of bringing the German Navy into 'complete and everlasting disrepute, by this monstrous thing' went some way towards retribution, but I wanted some bugger's head. Someone should have been held accountable. Also, where was Hasler? Surely his presence at the trial would have had some effect? I felt he had let the lads and me down. Had he been there with me, at least we could have faced those responsible for the murder of our comrades together. I felt terribly alone.

Chapter 11

The Movie

Back at work once again in the plastics factory, I started to contemplate just what the future might have in store for me. I must admit, I didn't see much excitement on the horizon. Then, one evening, I got a phone call that brought a fresh challenge, and not a little glamour, into my dull grey life. The voice at the other end of the phone was that of a film producer, or so he said he was. Frankly, I found it hard to believe. The man was saying that he was involved with a company that was considering making a film of Operation Frankton. They would call it *Cockleshell Heroes*. Not believing what I was hearing, and thinking it was some kind of joke, I told the caller he was a poor excuse for a comic and to leave me alone. The line went dead before I even had the chance to ask his name.

A few days later I received a letter from the mystery caller explaining that as he couldn't seem to get me to take him seriously on the phone, he thought he had better write. He said his name was Alberto Broccoli (known to all as 'Cubby') and he assured me he was a *bona fide* film producer and that he was acting under instructions from Mr. Irving Allen of Warwick Film Productions who made British films for Columbia Pictures. The letter went on to say, would I please call him and make an arrangement for a time and place to meet to discuss the project. Wow! The guy was for real. I phoned right away and made an appointment to meet the producer on the following Saturday at his office.

During our meeting, Cubby Broccoli outlined the procedure to me. The film was to be shot in Portugal. The river scenes would be filmed on the River Tagus – which in its topography closely resembles that of the Gironde. Also, good weather could practically be guaranteed in Portugal, unlike in France, where delays due to climatic change could prove to be extremely expensive. Almost as expensive, Cubby informed me, as the prices charged by French trades people, when they realized a film company was in the area! My job would be to accompany the film unit wherever they were shooting and answer any questions put to me connected with the raid. My old boss on Operation Frankton, Colonel Hasler, was to be similarly engaged. Having got leave of absence from my job at the plastics works, I waited patiently for the call to join the film unit. The wait was further frustrated by the project being post-poned several times – so much so that I began to think that it would never take place. Then the call came, giving me just two days notice to be in readiness for a car that would collect and convey me to Heathrow airport, where I was to board a plane and fly to Portugal. Whew!

After landing at Lisbon and clearing customs, I was met by a courier who drove me to the hotel where a reservation had been made for me. On checking in, I was pleased to find that most of the cast of the film were also staying at the same hotel. Hopefully, I would get the opportunity to meet them. I was not disappointed; they were a wonderful crowd of actors. The young man who was to play me was Anthony Newley (practically unknown then). It would be impossible to find a more likeable lad – he kept us laughing all day long. The rest of the cast was equally likeable. Apart from Tony, of course, my firm favourite was the co-star Trevor Howard. He had a wonderful sense of humour and was most sociable.

The other star of the film was that wonderful actor, José Ferrer. I found him to be very agreeable, but he wasn't too popular with the other actors. His persona lightened somewhat when his lovely wife, the singer Rosemary Clooney, visited. She was an instant hit with all the men-folk and not least with my colleagues from the 1st SBS who were on loan from the Royal Marines to do the canoeing and underwater swimming scenes. They all adored her.

The SBS boys had their moment too when, during a film sequence involving canoes, Corporals Richens and Close rescued Trevor Howard and David Lodge after their canoe had capsized, saving them from almost certain death by drowning.

During the weeks that followed, I often wondered why I had been asked to be a technical adviser, since they never took any notice whatsoever of suggestions, or any criticism, made by either myself or Colonel Hasler. The answer was always 'Your ideas are welcome, but they would not work in the theme of things.' I suppose we were there because our names would look good on the film credits – implying authenticity. It didn't take us long to get the message, then we just lay back in the glorious sunshine and observed.

The shooting in Portugal completed, the unit returned to England for the filming around the marine barracks in Southsea and the scenes that were to be shot in the London docks. Hasler and I were not really needed for any of this, but it was good publicity for the film if we were still seen hanging around.

Eventually, the filming came to an end and the unit was disbanded. The producers, directors and technicians went on to other projects, whilst the young actors waited for that all-important phone call and the offer of a part that would further their careers. For me it was back to the plastics factory. Cheers!

Finally, the day arrived that I had so long looked forward to, the British premier of the film *Cockleshell Heroes*. Bryan Forbes and Richard Maibaum had written the screenplay and Phil Samuel produced it for Irving Allen and Alberto Broccoli. José Ferrer directed it himself.

In my hired dress suit and puffing away on a fag, I paced up and down in the front room of my home. I waited anxiously for the car that I had been promised would convey me to the Empire Theatre in Leicester Square. It seemed an eternity before the gleaming limousine arrived and when it did, boy did I feel important sitting in the back being chauffeur driven. 'King' for a night. As we approached Leicester Square, throngs of people had already gathered – waiting to catch a glimpse of the stars and dignitaries. My car was brought to a halt several times by people peering in to see who the occupant was. The look of disappointment on their faces when they found no one of any importance inside was amusing. Eventually my car was able to draw to a halt outside the theatre. I got out, straightened myself up, then walked into the theatre, passing through a guard of honour mounted by Royal Marines – a proud and memorable moment for me.

I was ushered inside the theatre and lined up with the stars of the film to be presented to His Royal Highness, The Duke of Edinburgh, Captain General of the Royal Marines, and his uncle, my old wartime boss, Lord Louis Mountbatten. When Prince Philip got around to me, we had quite a chat. Introductions over, it was time to go in to see the film. Although I had viewed some of the 'rushes' in Portugal, I was really excited at the prospect of viewing the complete version.

I must admit that I was very satisfied with the movie; in fact everyone seemed to enjoy it except Hasler. He couldn't enjoy it, because he wasn't there! He had written to David Astor (close friend of Hasler and at that time editor of *The Observer*) proffering some excuse about having to be out of the country at the time. His mother got to hear of this and wrote him a stiff letter saying that if he said he would be abroad at the time of the film premier, then he had better be. On 16 November 1955 Hasler, heeding his mother's words, took the cross channel ferry from Dover and spent the night of the film premier drinking in a French cafe.

The film was well received by the media. The *Daily Mail* said:

"No ordinary film would command such an audience and this is no ordinary film. It is one, which honours the Royal Marines and gives them no more honour than is their due."

The Royal Marines' Association, to whose benefit the receipts for the night – some £6000 – were donated, had sold out all seats for the premier within fourteen days of issue and five weeks before the performance. The evening was rounded off with a magnificent display given by young bandsmen of the Royal Marines; it made me feel so proud to have served in the 'Royals'.

Quite naturally, many of the invited guests gathered in the reception room eager to speak to the Prince, who was moving from person to person making polite conversation – a function he always carries out so well. A wonderful gentleman approached me and I recognized him at once; he was an old favourite of mine; none other than Douglas Fairbanks Jnr. I discovered that he was chairman of the *Cockleshell Heroes* fund and was responsible also for the publicity of the film. He said that he would like me to travel to America, where the film's release was imminent and follow it around – making personal appearances and giving interviews to press, radio and TV. I was over the moon at the idea and told him so. I was ready to go right there and then.

In the meanwhile *Cockleshell Heroes* had its premier in France. In fact, in Bordeaux, which couldn't have been a more fitting place to hold it. It was another gala night and after the film was screened, to much applause I might add, I was invited onto the stage and introduced to the audience. Then, Monsieur DuBois, the farmer and resistance member who had helped us escape, joined me on the stage and holding out his open hand said, 'Mr Sparks, I think this belongs to you?' Sitting in his upturned palm was the identity disc he had taken from my neck, when he sheltered Blondie and me during our escape. I never thought I would see that disc again. The Frenchman embraced me warmly, kissing me on both cheeks. I was moved beyond words – I could think of nothing to say to convey to him my gratitude for what he had done for me during those dark days. With a lump in my throat, I answered, 'I owe you my life'. Monsieur DuBois responded with, 'It has been a wonderful evening, but such a shame that Colonel Hasler isn't here to share it with all of us.'

Yet once more I paced the floor of my front room waiting for a car; when it arrived it was even bigger than the one I had ridden to the film premier in. I thought 'everything is big in America and it feels like it is starting right here for me.' I hoped I wasn't to be disappointed. Late that evening, I boarded the night plane to New York and a whole new set of experiences.

Accompanying me on the flight was a beautiful young singer named Yana, who had a small but evocative part in the film. Also travelling with us was Helen Cherry, the delightful wife of Trevor Howard, who was already in the States awaiting our arrival. It was a good flight, but having been allocated a sleeping compartment, I took advantage of it and slept most of the way.

When morning came, a stewardess wakened me with a lovely English breakfast but before I had finished the meal, we were circling over Manhattan, a wonderful sight when first you see it. Trevor Howard, together with one of the producers, met us off the plane and somehow whisked us through customs. I was certainly travelling first class.

I spent my first day in America – in bed. I had picked up a bug somewhere and needed a doctor, who gave me a few injections, which were rather painful, but did the trick. I was soon back on my feet and raring to see the sights. The following day I met two more people from Columbia Pictures who also were to travel with the unit and one of them was allotted to me as my 'agent'. His name was Jim and he was a wonderful man whom I immediately took to.

108

I knew from that very first meeting that we would become firm friends. He looked after me like a father, but along the way I did give him a few headaches!

I am always eager to explore new places and this was to be no exception. When Jim called at the hotel to collect me, I was nowhere to be found, so he searched downtown New York and was on the point of contacting the police, when suddenly I turned up. He wasn't best pleased; in fact he was in a state of panic. When I told him where I had been, he was even more cross. It seemed that I had found my way to the Bronx where one is in danger of being 'rolled' just for the fun of it. Jim made me promise never to go out alone again.

After a couple of days we were back on a plane bound for Toronto in Canada. With snow thick on the ground our plane touched down – the temperature was below freezing, but it didn't deter the boys from the press. They were out in force and waiting on the edge of the apron where our plane was now standing. A cordon of police with half a dozen squad cars was also there to escort us. As we walked towards the terminal building amid a continual barrage of flash bulbs firing, the chief of police greeted us. I was escorted to his car. Then, with police motor cycle outriders escorting us with lights flashing and sirens wailing, we drove through the streets of Toronto. I had always dreamed of what it might be like to be driven in such fashion, but actually to experience it was unreal.

We arrived at the Hotel St David and, after bidding farewell to some of our police escort, I was led away to the lounge in which a press conference had been arranged. I began wondering just who it was that they wanted to interview? When I found out that it was in fact me, and that I was the cause of all this media attention, I was staggered. Pressmen can be vicious and pull no punches – they have a nasty habit of putting words into one's mouth. I had to be very careful when answering a myriad of questions; they really wanted to print what was assumed and not what was actually said – always looking for something controversial. They asked where Colonel Hasler was, and once again, I made a plausible excuse for his absence.

The premier in Toronto was a massive affair; with searchlights making circles in the crisp, clear night sky. The radio stations constantly promoted the film and people turned out in their thousands. Walking onto the stage of the theatre to tumultuous applause, I quite naturally wondered who they were applauding. Then, looking around and realizing I was the only one standing there, thought, 'Blimey, it must be me'. A feeling of elation and humility swept through me, and it took a nerve-racking moment to collect my senses. Then I called upon my experience of standing before large gatherings at trade union meetings; it helped me out.

After the film was shown, I was asked to stand in the foyer and answer questions about it from the public. I was amazed at the daft questions some people asked, but after a time got used to it all. I was quite enjoying it really, then my agent Jim, said enough was enough and extricated me from the throng. From there we went on to a night-club to sample the entertainment – and of course a few beers!

The following day we flew back to New York. This was now our HQ where the planning for the rest of the road shows would take place.

Our next stop was Washington, where the local Columbia Pictures public relations man hit on a novel idea. He would hide me in a hotel for a week, whilst a competition ran in the newspapers to 'find the Cockleshell Hero'. Anyone recognizing me would be paid $100. Of course, no one was going to find me tucked away in a hotel, were they? I languished in comfort, but was even becoming bored with luxury, when at the end of a week, Jim collected me and together we walked through the streets of the city. Free at last, I hadn't walked far when I felt a tap on my right shoulder. Turning to face the person responsible, I was confronted by a man who challenged me with 'Sir, I think that you are the Cockleshell Hero.' I tried to fob him off by becoming slightly angry and telling him that I wasn't and accusing him of being rude. But he was having none of it. He could smell the $100 and stuck to his guns. By this time a crowd had gathered, so there was nothing left for me to do except admit that yes, I was the Cockleshell Hero.

Accompanied by the gaggle of pressmen who seemed to follow me wherever I went, Jim and I took the successful sleuth to the nearest cinema. Imagine my surprise when I found out that my captor was in fact an Englishman, who had not only just lost his job (he had my sympathy) but his surname was German. This made a wonderful headline in the following morning paper; it read 'Cockleshell Hero captured by German after years of evasion'.

The film gala was a splendid affair. The Washington dignitaries turned out in force. The traditional cocktail party followed. By now I was getting used to it – it wasn't too painful!

We returned to New York, settled down for a few days, then it was off once more. This time our destination was San Diego on the west coast where there is a huge naval base and a large contingent of US Marines. We would be sure of a warm welcome here.

Yana came with me on a visit to the marine training establishment where they treated us like royalty. Trainees are not allowed off the base, so when they saw Yana they went wild. And when she sang to them, she stole their hearts.

The night of the premier in San Diego was another thing. Just before we left the hotel for the theatre, there was a knock on the door of my room. When I opened it, standing before me was the biggest marine I had ever seen in my life. He quietly informed me that he was my personal escort and had been detailed to look after me.

As I walked from the hotel I got another shock. Searchlights were sweeping the sky and a huge tank was waiting for me. I mounted the mighty iron beast and, sitting up on the gun turret, I waved to the crowd as we moved off. Following behind in a Jeep and attracting a great deal of attention was the lovely Yana.

Another huge crowd had gathered at the theatre to greet us. Such was the enthusiasm of the people it took me a quarter of an hour to get inside of the building. The film was received very well indeed and when it was over, yet again I found myself standing on a stage, only this time I was surrounded by more top brass from the US Marine Corps than I had previously encountered. I stood with Trevor Howard and we were both interviewed by one of the top US disc jockeys.

After the ordeal we were once again whisked away to the ubiquitous cocktail party, not retiring until the early hours of morning, then having to rise again, after practically no sleep, to catch a plane back to New York. This was to be the pattern I would follow during the next six months.

Back in New York the merry-go-round started over, only this time we headed for Salt Lake City. We seemed to travel everywhere by aeroplane; the Americans caught them like we do buses. I used to love flying, but now I felt as though I were tempting providence. I was travelling alone, Trevor had an appointment in Mexico to negotiate terms for another film and Yana had stayed behind to attend an audition.

The plane touched down and taxied to the dispersal bay. As I descended the steps of the aircraft I could see my reception committee was a formation of men, the American version of our British Legion. Strange though it might seem, they were in fact all British. I was escorted to my hotel to give yet another press conference. I was beginning to get as much publicity as the President! Afterwards and during a refreshment break, I was able to meet the men who had formed my guard of honour and thank them personally for going to so much trouble for little old me.

In Salt Lake City I appeared on numerous radio and television shows, all publicising the film of course. The constant travelling, press calls and interviews began to take their toll. We were putting in eighteen hours per day. It is little wonder that so many film stars suffer from exhaustion with these hectic schedules. After three days we left for New York, where there was a brief stop before we flew down to Los Angeles. This was Hollywood and I loved it. Although our film was not due to be screened locally for some time, I was kept busy with newspaper interviews and radio and television shows.

From LA we went to New Orleans, where once again I had a police escort with wailing sirens. I rode with none other than the chief of police himself, which gave me the opportunity to invite him and the escort to a private party in my room. Here I must admit to having another agenda. I was intending asking the chief if there was any chance of my going out on patrol with his policemen. I was not a little surprised, but thrilled by his reaction to my request. 'Bill, we would love to have you with us. You can ride with two of my boys on night patrol. I will arrange it.'

Later, the very same evening, a police patrol car called for me. One of the two officers gave me a shotgun but warned me not to use it except in a dire emergency. I prayed for one! We hadn't been on the road for long when a warning light on the dashboard flashed. This meant the officers were being called to an incident. The radio informed us that a knife fight was taking place in a café. With sirens blaring and blue lights flashing we sped off through the streets of New Orleans to the incident. I was feeling great. Then a screech of brakes and we were outside the café. Even before the car had come to a complete standstill, one officer was out and running across the sidewalk towards the building. His colleague closely followed him, and I wasn't far behind either of them. I was not going to miss the chance of the possibility of any action. As we burst into the café, we could see that things were already under control. We had been beaten to the incident by another car. An officer had the would-be knifeman against a wall and was punching him in the face; the knife lay on the ground where the offender was soon to join it! Then, with their prisoner handcuffed and bundled into the back of their patrol car, the arresting officers left the scene.

The excitement over, we continued our patrol duties. We sighted a speeding car and gave chase. With lights flashing and sirens wailing we sped along the highway.

The car we were pursuing was no match for ours and soon we were alongside signalling the speeding driver to pull over. As he made to, he wound down the window and in a state of panic shouted, 'My wife is about to give birth. I am rushing her to hospital.' With sirens still screeching we escorted the expectant father and his wife to the maternity hospital. I am pleased to say we were in time.

After leaving the hospital we were cruising along the highway when the warning light flashed again. The officers were told to proceed silently to a car parking lot where three men had been observed pilfering from cars. We hastened along to the lot and swung the car around to block the entrance. My colleagues were out of the car in a flash and running around the lot, with me close on their heels. We sighted the culprits and they saw us, whereupon the offenders made off in different directions. I thought lovely, one each! We then entered into a proper game of cat and mouse. I followed my man around by using the sound his boots were making on the concrete. He must have cottoned on to my tactics, as things suddenly went quiet. He had obviously decided to lay low.

Cautiously, I crept around the cars, listening for the slightest sound that would indicate where the villain lay. I hoped that he wasn't armed. Then, coming around the back of a car, I saw my desperado. Suddenly I wasn't at all sure what to do. I mean, I wasn't supposed to be there, not officially that is. But then he didn't know that, did he? In my most authoritarian voice I commanded him to stay still and put his hands on his head. Thankfully and much to my relief, he did just that. Having made an arrest I was overjoyed and, when my colleagues each appeared with a man in tow, I was doubly pleased because we had made a clean sweep. A police van was summoned to take the offenders to the police station, and we followed. After my police officer colleagues had interrogated the prisoners and formerly charged them, we continued with our patrol.

The officers decided to take a look around an area occupied mainly by blacks. Although it was in the early hours of the morning there was still plenty of activity. As our car, with headlights blazing, slowly turned each corner, groups of men could be seen scurrying away in the shadows. They had been gambling and could smell a police car when it arrived in the vicinity. We decided to make a raid. Increasing speed and turning a corner on two wheels suddenly the car's headlamps picked up a group of men gambling.

As we screeched to a halt, the gamblers fled. Undeterred, my colleagues and I jumped from our car and chased the men up various alleyways. They were too quick for us and most got away, although we did catch one. I was surprised that my colleagues seemed to know all the gamblers by name; the one we caught was no exception. They questioned him in much more of a jovial than hostile way, and I soon learnt that these street-wise hustlers were masters of the question and answer game. Nothing could be proved so we had to let him go.

It was getting light and our tour of duty was coming to an end. I was feeling disappointed, it was all over too soon – I had really enjoyed the experience. We finished our patrol 'inspecting' a night-club. Here again the two officers were well known; the manageress came to join us and they were on first name terms with her – the drinks and entertainment were free. I got the feeling that my chums were regular visitors to this establishment!

My new-found friends returned me to my hotel where reluctantly I bade farewell to two fine coppers. I managed to get a few hours sleep before being aroused by Jim, my agent, to continue with the task of promoting the film. I was invited to meet the mayor by whom I was suitably entertained and given the freedom of the city. After the usual round of media shows and a personal appearance at yet another gala performance of the film, it was time for us to leave the good friends we had made. Soon we were aboard another plane, this one heading towards San Francisco.

San Francisco is a beautiful city, with so much to see, if only I could get the chance to savour it. To be fair the film company always tried their level best to cram as much sightseeing into my program as possible. I managed to take in Chinatown and ride a cable car to the top of Nob Hill. Doesn't everyone? The highlight of my stay was a party which was held on top of the highest building in the city, called 'Top of the Mart' where on a revolving seat one could take in the magnificent view of the Golden Gate bridge and the prison island called Alcatraz (still very much in use at that time).

After the showing of the film, where once again I made a personal appearance, I was escorted onto the stage by a squad of American marines. I think they must have been especially selected – the smallest being over six feet tall. The marines insisted that I 'run ashore' with them and so I found myself in a sleazy dive packed with sailors. I knew exactly what to expect; fighting with matelots is traditional and I was not to be disappointed. In time honoured fashion a sailor threw a snide comment at a marine and away it went. Thankfully, I was not too involved in this battle. When things began to get a bit warm, I was grabbed by two marines, who put me in a car and drove me back to my hotel. I never did discover the outcome of the scrap. I hope we won!

We flew to Baltimore. I was not impressed with this place; it was too industrialized. But I did get to meet the mayor who bestowed on me the freedom of the city. Next stop was Chicago, not an impressive place either – at least I thought not. We only stopped for television shows and radio interviews. I was beginning to get more airtime than a professional performer! The few days spent here ended with a spectacular party for all those involved in the Columbia Pictures publicity machine. They certainly loved spending the company's money.

Next we flew to Portland, then on to Dallas – a pretty town surrounded by hills, cowboy country. From here we travelled back to Washington then on to New York. Despite the superb hospitality I had been shown by the American people I was getting extremely tired of travelling. I had been on the circuit for six months – alone for the last two, the faithful and lovely Yana having dropped out of the race leaving me to carry on. When it was suggested that we fly down to Las Vegas, I thought that it was time to lay my cards on the table (excuse the pun). I had decided that I was not going to continue with the publicity tour. The wanderlust in me had been cured – for a time anyway.

Wearily and regrettably I bade farewell to my agent, dear old Uncle Jim. We had become very close friends during the past six months and I was genuinely sad to be leaving him. But it was time to go. I boarded a plane for England and slept during most of the long flight home. When we touched down at Heathrow airport the nostalgia hit me and I was glad to be home.

I followed the careers of all those who appeared in the film. I was especially saddened when the lovely Yana died at an early age from cancer. Her career had gone slowly downhill and she ended up working behind the counter at a branch of Boots the Chemist. Tony Newley, whom I had also grown close to, also died of the dreaded disease, but much later. The last time I saw him was when he invited me to a performance of the hit musical *Scrooge* where he was playing the lead. My wife Renie and I went back to his dressing room after the show. Tony wrote these words on my programme: 'Bill I am so proud to be your friend'. I can't begin to tell you how proud I am to be thought of by him in that way. Not so long after our last meeting the dear man died. Thankfully, I will always have them with me on film. When I hear Yana sing *The London I Love,* it still brings a lump to my throat.

Dear God, may both the lovely Yana, and the irrepressible Tony, find the peace they so richly deserve.

I was disappointed by the lack of support from my old CO Colonel Hasler. I know he never liked the film, and especially not the title. But he was happy to take the film company's money as an adviser. He seemed to place principle over loyalty, but that seemed to go out of the window when money was involved.

After a few days rest at home, I returned to the plastics factory. Everything seemed so incredibly dull. I thought it time to move on and seek alternative employment. The question I asked myself was, 'what, if anything, would induce me to settle down?' I tried taking out an insurance agent's book, but very soon came to the realization that I was not cut out for the insurance business, although working for myself did have its appeal. I then became an ice-cream vendor, but failed, on account of giving away more ice-cream than I actually sold – mostly to poor kids. I ended up with a deficit instead of a profit. That was the end of that. Fortes ice-cream parlours need not have worried about competition from me!

There seemed nothing better on the horizon than my old job of bus driving, so with some misgivings, I returned to it. I had to go through the procedure of application and interview again, but there it was. I was re-engaged as a driver and for most of the time was quite content. I got the odd break here and there when the film company asked me to travel to the continent to promote the film. The bus company was very considerate about my occasional absences and welcomed my application to become an inspector.

I passed the prescribed exam and became a bus inspector. This meant that I would jump on and off buses at random inspecting tickets. I also had to stand at various checkpoints and time buses. The job was all right in summer months but when winter set in my old chest problem from the war days began to rear its head. Having had bronchial pneumonia, my chest was very weak and I was now getting sustained bouts of bronchitis every winter. I thought I had better do something about getting an inside job, so applied for the position of garage inspector. I passed another exam and was duly promoted. It meant that from here on I would be working on the inside of the garage and not on the outside, a much better prospect.

A BBC producer named Tom Waldron, who said he had been commissioned to write a book on Operation Frankton, approached me asking would I agree to collaborate with him on it. I said that I would be glad to. Very soon after I had had this conversation I was approached by Brigadier Lucas-Phillips, a military historian and author, as he too was writing an account of the raid. He said Blondie Hasler had already agreed to collaborate with him on the project and would I? I told him that I had recently made a commitment to Tom Waldron, which he respected, and so was unable to help him. Unfortunately Tom dragged his heels, and Lucas-Phillips easily beat us to publication. Although the book Cockleshell Heroes was a huge success, and a very good book it is I might add, I was saddened because I didn't get the chance to have any input on the story. It was pointless Tom Waldron continuing with our version – the day was lost.

The film was extremely successful all over Europe, America, and Canada. It is still quite regularly shown on TV here. The book was reprinted many times selling over a quarter of a million copies. Someone made a great deal of money out of the story (I certainly didn't), but it's a pity they didn't show themselves when I was trying to get recognition for the lads who gave their lives, for they were the real Cockleshell Heroes. As it was I fought a lone crusade and, but for the much valued help from my MP, Sir Bernard Braine whom I wrote to on 14 July 1980 I doubt anything would have been done. He was marvellous but it still took some time before anything was achieved. Sir Bernard wrote to me on 23 January 1984 saying:

'What I did in regard to the monument was done because I was struck by your own dedication to the memory of your dead comrades, and by the courage and initiative shown by you all, and the fact that unless we did something tangible to put the record straight the whole story would not be known. With the monument at Poole, we have the assurance that the story will be known for all time.'

Sadly, Blondie Hasler played no part in the long and protracted struggle to get a monument to our comrades erected, although he was there when it was unveiled.

Mary Lindell, Comtesse de Milleville died in 1987 and on 13 February a service of thanksgiving was held in France. I attended (wild horses would not have kept me away) and it was a most moving occasion evoking in me memories of the most courageous lady I have ever had the privilege of knowing. Both Hasler and I owed our lives to her. Sadly Hasler was not there to honour and thank this remarkable woman. I know he had been ill, although he did attend the funeral of one of his contemporaries not long after Mary's death. Blondie Hasler died on 5 May 1987. I left my hospital bed to attend his memorial service.

Chapter 12

A Book and a Painting

It was 1986 and I was sixty-four years of age. I had taken the ferry to the Isle of Wight to see once more the area where we had performed our supposed boom patrol duties. It was on the return journey that I noticed this lovely blonde with a smile that would melt an iceberg. I tried to engage her in conversation. At first she seemed reluctant but became more amenable as we neared the mainland. She told me her name was Renie and that she lived on the island, but was on her way to visit her daughter. I managed to get her phone number and was determined to pursue her. Not only did I follow my intention but within six months I had married her. The best day's work I ever did!

Unfortunately my health was deteriorating around this time. It was my chest mainly that was giving me problems. It had got worse with each winter, causing me to take more and more time off from work. This just wasn't me. I have never been a shirker and I didn't like it. I had to face things, and consider retirement.

Following one particular visit to hospital a doctor confirmed that my condition was due to war service, and suggested I apply for a war disability pension. After thorough investigation, and although the Ministry of Defence did accept that my recurring bronchitis was due to my military service, and that the incident when I fell into the sea whilst stationed in Iceland was a contributory factor, the grade I now fell into did not entitle me to a war pension. Thanks for nothing!

With little option I gave notice of my intention to retire to London Transport, my employers, and did so. I had often wondered how I would cope with inactivity after a lifetime in harness. I soon came to wonder, as many do, how I ever had time

119

to go to work! I didn't miss it one bit. I found plenty to do around the house and in the garden, but most of all I had time to enjoy the company of my lovely wife.

Like many other retired couples, we began dreaming of living in the country, away from the rat race, although Canvey Island where we then lived couldn't exactly be described as such. The country appealed to both of us and after some careful consideration we decided that with the sale of our bungalow, we could just about afford a place in Sussex, the county we preferred.

Those who experience it can only appreciate the disappointments and heartbreak that go with selling property We had selected the site and put a deposit on the property that we desired and just when we should have been moving, the prospective buyers of our bungalow pulled out of the deal. This really left us in a hole, forcing us to reduce the asking price of our property so as to effect the quick sale we now desperately needed. Eventually we moved into our Shangri-La. We didn't have a care. Although money would be tight, we would manage.

We were blissfully happy, that is until our elected government decided that working class people should not be so, and reduced my state pension by £20 per week. This, they said, was because I was in receipt of a pension from my last employer. The pension they referred to was a scheme that I had made a voluntary contribution to, and which now yielded a meagre weekly sum. A reduction of £1,000 per year in income, was more than we could stand.

Renie and I spent hour after hour racking our brains trying to find ways to economize. We weren't exactly living an extravagant lifestyle in the first place, so economies were difficult to identify. Something would have to be sold, but what? The only single item of any real value we owned was my Distinguished Service Medal. I couldn't possibly sell that, could I? We discussed possible alternatives but none seemed feasible, so with great reluctance I approached the auctioneers Sotheby's. The famous auction house agreed to put my treasure into a forthcoming sale. It was with a heavy heart that I handed my DSM into their safekeeping.

Some days later, on picking up a daily paper, I was astonished to see a photograph of myself accompanied by a text which stated that Bill Sparks the 'Cockleshell Hero' was having to sell his DSM to make ends meet. I had no idea that my action would bring such attention from the media. I received dozens of letters of support from the public, some even offering financial help, which I couldn't accept of course. There was one unsavoury offer of help from a 'friend' who through his company would make up the monthly shortfall in my pension, but in return he wanted the deeds of our home. Some friend!

The Royal Marines Museum sent a retired major to see me. He slapped a cheque book on my kitchen table and said, 'Right Sparks, how much do you want? I am not leaving here without your medal.' He offered £11,000. As much as I would have loved to see my DSM end up in the corps museum, I had already committed myself to Sotheby's (who had also indicated my medal would fetch in excess of £12,000) and in turn, they had published their catalogue, with a photograph of me on the front cover. To break my agreement with the auction house would have cost me at least £2,000. I told the major I could not accept his offer, and he went off in a huff.

Come the day of the auction my wife and I were escorted into a private room until the main item of the day, my medal, Lot 208, came up. I was grateful to be out of the limelight and away from the many newsmen hanging around. After some brisk bidding my DSM was knocked down for £31,000. The anonymous bidder made his bids by phone. The under-bidder was the Royal Marines Museum. Had the Museum not been so pompous and offered a more realistic price when they sent their representative to see me before the auction, I am sure we could have come to an agreement.

I was besieged by TV and newspaper reporters who, according to them, said how lucky I had been to achieve such a result. All I know is that Renie and I could now sleep peacefully in our bed, knowing we were out of the money problem our considerate government had landed us with. As much as I was saddened at parting with my cherished possession, without a home, where could I have kept it? Anyway, I now had someone I cherished even more – my lovely wife Renie.

A colonel from the Royal Marines, in an act of petulance, told both TV and news reporters that, in light of not securing the medal for the Corps' Museum, he would dismantle the Cockleshell display that was exhibited there.

The publisher Leo Cooper, approached me. Leo said he would be interested in publishing a book of my account of Operation Frankton. With the fiftieth anniversary not too far away it seemed like a good idea to me and I told him so. I set about things with my old typewriter, and whilst I found recollecting the events of that hazardous operation fulfilling, I found, and still do, reliving the incidents where we lost our comrades very emotional.

When I had finished writing my memoirs Leo introduced Michael Munn who was to co-operate with me on the final manuscript. I was quite pleased with the finished book which sold [rather] well. It has since been published in paperback. A prerecorded tape was made with George Sewell reading my story. He did an excellent job, and I was really pleased with it. The firm that produced the tape did so in a series of escape stories called *Great Escapes* but sadly went bust, hence I received very little in royalties.

It was through Leo Cooper that I met the England and Gloucestershire cricketer Jack Russell. Jack is also an accomplished artist and Leo suggested Jack paint a commemorative picture of Operation Frankton, a similar project to one he had done for the St Nazaire Society. Jack came down to Crowborough, where I lived at the time (we have since moved to East Sussex) with his agent Jim Ruston. There began a friendship that survives to this day. Renie and I grew especially close to Jim, like me a cockney. We have so much in common.

When Jack finished the painting I was so impressed with it. I could feel the cold, cold water he had so brilliantly captured on canvas. The painting shows the five canoes as we enter the first tidal race, the last time my mates and I were together. It brought a lump to my throat. A limited edition of 850 prints was published and I countersigned every one, which gave me cramp, but I loved every minute of it. The original painting was shown to the public for the first time at the Imperial War Museum, and a number of top brass were there to view it. It was a splendid occasion, and I was deeply moved when Jack Russell presented me with a print, on the border of which he had drawn my portrait. It has pride of place in our home and is a constant reminder of my missing comrades.

Each summer Jim Ruston and his lovely wife Joyce invite Renie and me to their Gloucestershire home for a holiday. We so look forward to it. Jack Russell also invited us to watch Gloucestershire play Yorkshire in the Benson & Hedges Cup Final at Lord's cricket ground. We had a wonderful day, made all the more special by Gloucestershire's triumphant win over a shrewd adversary.

In December every year the French hold a memorial service at the Château Magnol in Blanquefort, where Mick Wallace and Jock Ewart were held prisoner. A plaque is fixed to the wall where these incredibly gallant marines were executed. The extensive bullet holes in the wall are testament to the savagery of their captors. The memorial service is well attended by French wartime veterans, the Mayor of Bordeaux, and other dignitaries – plus a military band. A party of Royal Marines from Poole, led by an officer, lay a wreath. The whole ceremony of remembrance is a moving and fine tribute to my comrades. In December 1999 George Ewart, the brother of my comrade Jock, attended the ceremony. It was his first visit to the place where his brother was murdered. George, quite naturally, was overcome with emotion, so I was pleased that Renie was there to comfort him. He is a lovely man, just like his brother.

I continue to do my best to keep alive the memory of those who paid the supreme sacrifice during those black days in December 1942. *They* are the 'Cockleshell Heroes', I am merely the proud spokesman for these exceptionally brave men.

Operation Frankton – from the German Viewpoint

Quite recently a gentleman called François Boisnier, who had served with the French special forces, contacted me. He said he was organizing a commemorative walk following our escape route from St Genès-de-Blaye to Ruffec. It would be named the *Frankton Walk*. He further stated that through a colleague he had managed to get, from the German military archives at Freiburg, copies of the signals that German forces defending the port of Bordeaux in 1942 had sent to each other during and after Operation Frankton. My friend and colleague Jim Ruston had them translated into English, and I reproduce those relevant here. They are reproduced as translated, except that the general comments in *italics* are mine with any explanatory remarks shown in brackets [ ]. You will see how, in a meticulous way, the Germans gradually worked out what we were up to.

Document 1

From: Operations Section, HQ 708th Division

In the following the division reports the arrest of two marines . . .

At 21.50 hours on 7/12/42, Major Beyer of Flak Division 999 reported to the Operations Officer [1A in the original] of the division:

Radar station W.310 has detected a ship 4km south-east of Pointe de Grave. No further information. [The ship spotted must have been HMS *Tuna*, whilst she was on the surface.]

21.55 hours: Order from Operations Officer to Battalion Soulac 'Increased vigilance . . .'

22.00 hours: Query from Operations Officer to Navy Artillery Division 284, Captain Panzel: 'What's the matter? Use searchlights.'

22.20 hours: Repeated query by Operations Officer to Captain Panzel. Answer: 'Nothing to be seen, searchlight seen about 8km away, sighting likely to have been a fishing boat that has lost its way.'

After this no further measures taken by division. No observations during the night.

At 12.45 hours on 8/12, Flak Division 595 Battalion Soulac called and reported:

'Two Anglo-American marines, soaking wet, have been arrested by us.' [Wallace and Ewart]

12.50 hours: Order by battalion to search the coast and the forest area behind the coast, at the same time report to regiment.

13.00 hours: Regiment reported the above information to Intelligence Officer [1C] of division adding 'Search action ordered. Prisoners to be delivered to the [the area's] naval command, as they are marines.' Subsequently a further order from Intelligence Officer to establish more details immediately. Especially: what branch of service they are, type of clothing, have any maps or documents been found, when and where arrested. Report immediately to Division.

15.40 hours: Battalion Soulac reported to Division:

At 06.00 hours two British marines in uniform approached the first aid post of the Fähren Flotilla (ferry boats) probably believing it to be a house occupied by a Frenchman. The soldiers have been arrested. They are being interrogated by the respective office. The result is not yet known here. Due to the incident the battalion has ordered that the coast be searched by troops. In addition a search of the coastal forest area is taking place.

16.00 hours: As report insufficient, query from Intelligence Officer to Area Navy Command: 'What was the result of the interrogation?' Adjutant Sea Command offered the following information. 'Possibly an explosives commando. A rubber dinghy, maps and explosives have been found. Kpt. Lt. Hattich of Defence Command Bordeaux will go to Le Verdon, where the prisoners have been taken from the northern bank, to carry out interrogation.

16.20 hours: After query from Intelligence Officer, Flak Division 595 reported: 'Interrogation not yet taken place. Will start immediately after the arrival of Kpt. Lt. Hattich, who is expected at any time.'

Further conversations took place between several officers regarding the above matters until after 17.00 hours when the phone line became intermittent, going dead for periods.

Around 18.00 hours Captain Rosenberger, Intelligence Officer, informed the Divisional Commander: 'At 05.45 hours on 8/12/42 two English marines looked for shelter at the first aid post of Flak Division 595, which they mistook for the house of a French civilian. After arrest they identified themselves as sole survivors of a warship which had been torpedoed during the night.'

'A search of the area discovered the following. At point W301 a rubber dingy, anchored several hundred metres out at sea. This has not yet been recovered due to heavy surf. At W320 a map of the Gironde estuary with colour marking of military positions, two aerial photographs of Bordeaux Submarine Bunker and other small items have been found.'

At the same time the Intelligence Officer asked the commander of Flak Division 595 why he had taken so long to report the capture of the marines. The commander of the Flak Division said he had believed that they were shipwrecked sailors, and only at around 12.00 hours, after finding the small boat, which was flooded during high tide, and not yet recovered by the Navy, did he realize that they might be a commando force, and informed Battalion Soulac. Apart from that he had informed Naval Command Gascony which was responsible for the interrogation of alleged shipwrecked prisoners.

The Naval Command did not in fact inform the Division.

The reason why the information was relayed so late is that it was not possible to obtain authentic documentation from the Navy and the Flak Division during lunch hours. *Super German efficiency – what?* During this time the prisoners were on their way from the southern bank to the northern bank and back again! Army units could not report any details as all the communications took place between the offices of the Flak Division and the Navy.

The Division:

1) Reproached the commander of Flak Division 595 that he did not immediately report the prisoners to the Battalion Commander Soulac, his immediate superior, or to the Division.

2) Gave strict orders to the Naval Command Gascony that in

future, any events, which might be in the least suspicious, were to be reported to Division at once.

3) The action of the Intelligence Officer, in informing the Divisional Commander only after the exact documentation had been obtained, was wrong. He should have reported anything he had without delay. This procedure has now been made clear.

While this report is being written, at 22.00 hours, the interrogation of the prisoners is still taking place. The result of the interrogation will be reported on the morning of 9/12/42.

Having had their 'shipwrecked sailors' alibi discredited, Mick Wallace and Jock Ewart had to think on their feet. Their subterfuge and the German Navy's early acceptance of it had already given us the vital hours necessary to penetrate the harbour at Bordeaux. Now the wonderful Mick invented another plausible story that was to give us valuable time to proceed on our mission. Jock Ewart playing dumb, was the perfect foil to Mick's inventiveness.

Document 2

708 J.D. Hauptmann Glatzel reported by phone at 03.52 hours on 9/12/42.
To: Intelligence Section, 708th Division

Interrogation result so far: The two captured Englishmen left Portsmouth about two weeks ago. Due to the bad weather the submarine cruised until yesterday evening, setting down the two early in the night, in a canoe, in the Bay of Biscay probably just outside the Gironde estuary. They were given a course, which they followed.

After some time they saw a fire and made towards it. In the morning at around 04.00 their boat capsized in the surf at Pointe de Grave. They say that they only just managed to save themselves. They went ashore, allegedly to give themselves up. They are wearing British uniforms, without headwear, consisting of a type of twill trousers and blouson, similar to a camouflage shirt. On their sleeves are rank and insignia, and the wording 'Royal Navy', plus badges for mixed enterprises, army, navy, air force.

In other words they were wearing Royal Marines' shoulder flashes and Combined Operations' badges, clearly denoting, right at the outset, that they were legitimate combatants, and thus protected by the Geneva Convention.

The prisoners allege their orders were to paddle at night and to hide during the day. They were to travel up the Gironde and fix explosives to German ships using the limpet mines they were carrying to cause explosions and sink the ships. They had maps of the Gironde up to Bordeaux as well as two aerial photographs dated November 1942. The maps are marked to show occupied and enemy-free territory. Magnets, and some ammunition, camouflage netting, and other items of equipment have been found. The capsized boat has not yet been recovered. Further investigation will only be possible during daylight and low tide. Then the interrogation will also continue.

The commander of submarine P49 only gave the attack orders to the two men once they were on board the vessel, and after it had been at sea for about a week. They belong to a troop of about fourteen men gathered together by the Navy at Portsmouth. This troop was put together about nine months ago. Apart from the two captured, the submarine was to deploy another two men, but this was aborted because the second canoe was damaged during the launch.

After carrying out their orders the two prisoners were somehow to make their way to unoccupied territory. They claim that they were not given any French papers nor addresses nor any money.

The leader of the enterprise (*Mick Wallace telling them he was boss*) is quite willing to give information, but the second man is reluctant to tell the truth, and claims not to have been informed about the purpose of the mission.

Document 3

From: Naval Command – Western France
Stamped by Naval Command Gascony.
Re: Sabotage in Bordeaux on 12 December 1942.

At 22.00 hours on 7/12/42 suspicious activity was detected in the Gironde estuary. A search using searchlights bore no result.

At 15.00 hours on 8/12 the Flak Division captured two British marines, who had drifted ashore in a boat, at Le Verdon. When interrogated on 8, 9 and 10 December it was established that they had been ordered to travel up the Gironde by canoe and fix limpet mines to ships on the Gironde. Both were shot as members of a sabotage unit on 11/12/42.

Mick and Jock still insisted they were alone. Magnificent.

On the morning of 12/12/42 the steamers *Alabama, Dresden, Tannenfels, Portland*, and the *Sperrbrecher* (flak ship) were damaged by explosive limpet mines fixed under water on their seaward sides. In the afternoon of 12/12/42 two canoes with sketches, limpet mines, air sacks, hand grenades, iron rations and some pieces of equipment were found near Blaye outside of Bordeaux and were secured.

On the basis of these findings it is concluded as follows:

Various sabotage units of two men each were deployed in canoes from submarines outside the Gironde estuary. Under the cover of darkness and using the strong currents they advanced into the Gironde and Garonne up to the port of Bordeaux without being noticed. Here they affixed explosives to the ships mentioned – approximately 1 metre below the waterline, and then went ashore below Bordeaux, after having sunk or abandoned their boats.

Document 4

Telegram: Secret Commando Matter
From: Navy Intelligence Service
To: Naval Command Gascony, received 14 December 1942
Re: Investigation concerning ship sabotage

Steamer **Alabama:** Five Explosions (07.00, 07.03, 08.00, 10.05 and 13.05 hours) All explosions on the waterside. 1st explosion at hatch 5; 2nd at hold 1; 3rd at hold 4 (without any visible damage); 4th near to rudder; 5th at stern . Explosions 1.5m below waterline. Hold 1 and 5 took in water. Ship is able to float; aft warp lines have been attached for safety reasons.

Steamer **Tannenfels:** Two explosions; 1st at approximately 08.30, second 30 seconds later (bigger explosion). Explosions on seaward side between holds 2 and 3 approximately 2.5m below waterline. Holds filled with water. Size of holes 1.0m × .6m. Leaks were sealed by divers, ship still floats, but is listing about 16 degrees.

Steamer **Dresden:** Two explosions (08.45 and 08.55 hours) hold 5 and hold 4. Leaks approximately 3–4m below waterline. Hold 5 and 4 filled with water, due to tear in the shaft tunnel, also holds

6 and 7. Size of leaks 1.25m × 0.85m. Stern of ship was immediately beached. Attempts to seal the leaks are being made.

Steamer **Portland**: Sentry felt slight vibration of ship at about 05.50 hours and 06.30 hours. 09.55 hours explosion at hatch 1, on seaward side, 1.0m to 1.5m below waterline. Water jet was seen. Hold 1 underwater leak approximately 0.5 × 0.4m. Sealing sail has to be attached, little reduction of water by pumping.

Sperrbrecher: Five explosions on seaward side at about 10.30 hours; no damage midship; it is assumed the mines fell off due to previous searching of the hull and then exploded later on the sea bed.

Document 5

From: LXXX Army Corps 14/12/42

18.10 hours: First Lt Willemer reported to his HQ at around 16.00 hours a 4.5 metre long canoe with green and black camouflage paint drifted ashore south of the Île de Re. There is no sign of the occupants. They were without doubt British sabotage troops who are now at large on the Re or near La Rochelle. HQ replied: Increased vigilance required. Secure Battery Cora during day and night with the strongest of methods.

Document 6

Secret Commando Matter
From: 708th Infantry Division
Re: Enemy acts of sabotage

On 17/12/42 two members of a British sabotage unit were taken prisoner in the district of Jonzac north of Bordeaux. From interrogation there is no doubt that there is a connection between these men and the acts of sabotage carried out on 12/12 against ships in Bordeaux harbour, and that the men taken prisoner in the area of the Gironde estuary on 8/12 also belonged to this sabotage unit. The British sabotage unit had a strength of approximately 13 men. They came by submarine with collapsible boats and then reached Bordeaux harbour with five boats by taking advantage of the flood tide. By attaching limpet magnetic explosives on ships some damage was caused.

They later admitted the not inconsiderable extent of the damage we inflicted.

Some eight or nine men from this sabotage unit are still free.

It is discouraging that this event could take place, even though units had been warned after the arrest of the first two saboteurs. This proves that there exists a certain carelessness in certain areas and that troops have not been instructed properly with regard to the danger of such enemy actions. Therefore the following has been ordered:

Each act of sabotage is to be communicated to all personnel so that each soldier knows what cunning methods of combat the enemy is using.

Sentry and patrol duties must not only be carried out according to the traditional methods, but greater versatility should be practised when on patrol. Unexpected checks, and raids and searches should be carried out. Special caution is required on holidays.

Acts of sabotage, attacks and even only the suspicion of sabotage must be reported to the relevant district headquarters as quickly as possible.

Offering suitable rewards for the prevention of acts of sabotage will promote initiative and attention to duty. On the other hand negligence must be punished very severely.

Future enemy attacks of this type will be prevented if soldiers are vigilant and the relevant district headquarters attentive to their duties.

Document 7

Defence Sub-division Bordeaux
Interrogation report 29/12/42

A. First Lieutenant MacKinnon Royal Marine, Portsmouth division. Born 15/7/21 in Oban Argyllshire/Scotland, living in Glasgow at 22 Clarendon Street.

B. Marine James Conway, belonging to the same division as A) born 28/8/22 in Stockport near Manchester, living in the same place.

Occurrence:

The two prisoners named above belong to the commando unit which carried out acts of sabotage in Bordeaux harbour during the night of 7/ and 8/12/42. The marine made a full confession, the officer is still refusing to answer questions. The sailor describes the occurrence as follows:

The commando consisted of volunteers from various divisions. Together with the officers it totalled 13 men. The training took place in Plymouth, where they were billeted in private houses. The crews were trained in rowing and swimming, in the use of light weapons, and in the attachment of limpet mines on ships, this was carried out in all weather conditions. At the end of September – beginning of October the men went for eight days to Gourock, one hour by train from Glasgow, where they received further training, and learnt to climb cliffs. They were accommodated on the depot ship 'Alrawdah'.

About three weeks before the mission the crew (2 officers and 11 men) were again brought to Gourock and received further training. On 30/11 or 1/12/42 they embarked with their boats and equipment on the submarine No. 94. The crew of this submarine allegedly consists of 40–50 men. The submarine travelled directly to the Gironde estuary, where it had to cruise for 2–3 days and go deep, allegedly because of bad weather.

The mission began on 7/12/42. One boat was holed while being taken out of the hold, and had to remain on board. Only five boats with two men in each started. No 13 was a reserve and he also remained on the submarine.

The orders for the mission were as follows:

To stay together as a group until the Gironde estuary was reached, then form two groups, one group being led by Major Hasler and the other by First Lieutenant MacKinnon. To paddle during the night and spend the days at certain points on the land (for this the crews had maps from which German positions on the banks of the Gironde could be determined). The mission was to be carried out in Bordeaux harbour during the third night after landing. If the boats got separated only the last part of the order applied: i.e. on the third day after landing to enter Bordeaux harbour during the hours of darkness on the flood tide, and attach limpet mines to large ships, if possible.

The following occurred: At the Gironde estuary one boat capsized due to strong currents, and Major Hasler helped the two crewmen (*Sheard and Moffat*) to get near the shore, from where they swam to it. Because of this incident the boats lost sight of each other. The whole group got separated and each boat had to continue on its own. The now captured crew maintain that they never saw their comrades again, not even in Bordeaux harbour.

After the execution of the mission the unit had been ordered not to go directly to the Spanish border, but to reach Spain via a detour. To accomplish this order they had been given the name of a village in the Bordeaux area, where they would find friends to obtain civilian clothes and guidance. For reasons of decency Marine Conway did not want to name the village. At present it was decided not to force him to do so, to avoid making him obstinate. However, he gave the following information:

His first lieutenant and he himself had an accident at the Bec d'Ambes near the confluence of the Garonne and Dordogne rivers during the last night before carrying out the mission. They ran into an obstacle in the water which they could not see in the darkness. The boat was holed, and sank. They were forced to abandon their boat together with explosives and the rest of its contents, except for the sack with the money, iron rations and maps. They were no longer in a position to continue with the mission. They had spent the night on the Île Cazeau, so swam back there. A fisherman rowed them in a small boat to the western bank of the Garonne, where they found help in Margeaux. The name of the village was given to everyone on the submarine as a place where they would find help. The prisoner claims that from here he and his lieutenant walked to La Reole. They walked for three days; during one night they slept in the open and during the second in a barn.

According to this statement the village with the helpful Frenchmen must be Margeaux. SD Bordeaux [SD = Sicherheitsdeinst – Security Service, or in other words the Gestapo] will find out about this village, but there are signs that the marine is trying to obscure the real name of the village to spare the Frenchmen. Another village, which might be a possibility, has already been taken into consideration. As Conway claims that a Frenchman brought them across the demarcation line, the whole story of the march to the demarcation line and the village of Margeaux is unlikely. It can be assumed that the two Englishmen very soon received civilian clothes and help, and that they reached the place where they crossed the demarcation line either by train or car, especially as the marine is wearing very light canvas shoes which show no signs of wear. The place where the demarcation line was crossed is allegedly near Langon.

They had their own maps for the route they had to cover in France. These maps were found on them and are not part of the earlier material.

The First Lieutenant carried together with his dog tags a Spanish 20 centavos coin on a piece of string. He claimed that this coin was a lucky mascot, but immediately got caught up in contradictions when asked for the origin of the coin. It can be assumed that this coin was a recognition sign.

The two Englishmen will be interrogated further by SD Bordeaux.
Signed: Hauptmann, Interrogation Section
Of Dulag Nord Wilhelmshaven

Document 8

From: Interrogation Section of Dulag Nord Wilhelmshaven (Naval Intelligence) 3/1/43

The demolition commandos embarked with six canoes on Monday 30 November 1942 in Holy Loch, Clyde estuary, opposite Gourock, on the submarine 'P' or 'N' 94 (*they never managed to identify the* Tuna *as being the sub that conveyed the raiders*).

The submarine travelled to the Bay of Biscay, via the Irish Sea, mainly on the surface. After passing Land's End it dived during the day. Information about the course not available. Around 20.00 hours on Monday 7 December 1942 the men and their canoes were put into the water and ordered to travel up the Gironde during the nightly flood tide and carry out ship demolition during the night of 11/12 December.

After passing Pointe de Grave the boats were to continue individually and should not attack jointly. The order was only made known to the crews aboard the submarine after departure, using maps and photographs (many of which have now been found and secured). The commandos were told of the importance of this mission; it was stressed that it was aimed at blockade runners. The presence of a large number of blockade breakers was assumed, the expected number varying between eight and twelve. The distribution of ships in the individual berths seemed unknown. Each canoe had eight mines on board. Of the two canoes aimed at each group of ships, one was to attach the mines to the downstream half of the ship's side and the other to the upstream half to assure a good distribution of the mines, even in darkness. Each boat was only to attach two mines on each ship, so that it could attack four ships; each ship would then have four mines attached, if the mission ran smoothly. The mines were to be attached to the seaward side, and only in very favourable tidal conditions was attachment on the pier side to be attempted. The canoes were to seek out the biggest ships in the group allocated to them, but no tankers. It seems that no other information was given about the ships to be attacked.

After the mission the demolition commandos were to paddle downstream during the night, then sink their canoes and try to escape to Spain via unoccupied areas of France.

Organisation

The leader of the mission was Major Hasler or Haslar (Royal Marines); deputy was First Lieutenant MacKinnon (Royal Marines). The boats did not have numbers, but fish names starting with 'C' (for commando?) The major's unit consisted of the boats 'Catfish' (Major Hasler and Marine Sparks), 'Conger' (Corporal Sheard and Marine Moffat), and 'Crayfish' (Corporal Laver and Marine Mills). The unit of the First Lieutenant consisted of the boats 'Cuttlefish' (First Lieutenant MacKinnon and Marine Conway), 'Coalfish' (Sergeant Wallace and Marine Ewart), and 'Cachalot' (Marines Ellery and Fisher). The two officers' boats 'Catfish' and 'Cuttlefish' were to attack the ships in Bordeaux west-side. The boats 'Conger' and 'Crayfish' were to attack the ships in Bordeaux east-side.

Execution of the mission

The approach by the submarine occurred without incident. The launching of the canoes started according to plan at around 20.00 hours on 7 December 1942 at a position about six paddling hours south-west of the Pointe de Grave, i.e. not at point (A) of the captured map. The points on the captured map (A) (B) (C) (D) (E) (F) (G) are tidal markers according to statements, using which the demolition troops were to devise their approach, and do not denote any navigation or landing points.

The fourth boat to be launched, 'Cachalot', was damaged during the lifting through the torpedo hatch and was not used; its crew remained on board the submarine. The other five boats started together and about one hour later saw some searchlights right ahead. After some three hours the boats were caught on three separate occasions in strong tidal currents.

The first boat to experience problems was 'Coalfish'. Its leader, Sergeant Wallace, became very seasick. It was detached and ordered to seek cover on land and carry out the mission (attack ships Bordeaux east-side) at a later date than the one agreed. The crewmen Wallace and Ewart surrendered at 05.30 hours on Tuesday 8 December at Le Verdon south of Pointe de Grave. They were interrogated by the defence divisions and the SD Bordeaux on 8, 9 and 10 December, during which the involvement of another canoe (later identified as 'Cachalot') as well as the equipment of the boats became known. The two under interrogation did not mention the involvement of the other four boats. The two canoes which were to attack the ships in Bordeaux east-side therefore were out of action.

Sometime after the detachment of 'Coalfish', at about 03.00 hours on 8 December the boat 'Conger' capsized and had to be given up. The accident occurred, according to a believable statement, near a lighthouse at Pointe de Grave, which was lit up. Corporal Sheard and Marine Moffat were dragged near (200–400m) to the shore by the boats 'Crayfish' and 'Catfish' and then dismissed in order not to jeopardize the mission. Their boat was sunk by First Lieutenant MacKinnon, who after this had no further connection with the other two boats. According to [a naval signal, reference given] of 28 December the body of Moffat was washed ashore on 17 December at base 'Fanny' south-west of Le Blois en Re. The whereabouts of Corporal Sheard are still unknown.

The canoe 'Cuttlefish' with First Lieutenant MacKinnon and Marine Conway ran aground at around 21.00 hours on 10 December on the eastern shore of the Île Cazeau a little way across from Bec d'Ambes after coming into contact with an iron obstacle, according to believable statements, before it reached its destination (ships Bordeaux west-side).

The explosives still on board were exploded. The crew fled, initially separately, with the help of French civilians from whom they also obtained civilian clothes, but were caught by French police on the other side of the demarcation line in La Reole on 18 December and were brought to Bordeaux for interrogation by the SD.

The canoe 'Crayfish' (crew Corporal Laver and Marine Mills) reached its target (ships at Bassens) according to plan and carried out explosions on two ships. According to believable statements five mines were attached to the upstream ship and three mines to the next ship downstream, all on the seaward side. The planned distribution of the eight mines was not carried out, because the demolition commando knew of the problem with the boat 'Conger' (crew Sheard and Moffat) and they wanted to sink at least one ship. The mines were attached between 22.00 and 23.00 hours British Winter Time. The duration of the ignition timers was eight hours, with a margin of error of two hours either way. 'Crayfish' then travelled downstream close to the western shore until Labarde (opposite Île Cazeau) where it reunited with 'Catfish' (Major Hasler and Marine Sparks). Both boats then travelled along the western shore until Ford Medor, crossed the river between the southern tip of Île Boucheau and the small island Fort Pate and landed separately just north of Baye. The crew of 'Crayfish' destroyed their boat and set off on their escape route, but were arrested on 14 December in La Garde on this side of the demarcation line by the French police and were then handed over to SD Bordeaux. They had not been supported by French civilians, but had been reported to the police, and they were still wearing khaki coloured special uniforms.

The crew of the sixth boat 'Catfish', the leader of the mission, Major Hasler, and Marine Sparks, seemingly carried out their orders (attack ships Bordeaux west-side), which were established by interrogation of the other prisoners, on three ships according to plan. The damage report showed maximum two explosions per ship, which can be explained, as Major H did not know of the absence of First Lieutenant MacKinnon with 'Cuttlefish'. On the other hand H knew of the absence of the canoes 'Cachalot' and 'Coalfish' which were aimed at the ships Bordeaux east-side, and of the absence of one of the canoes aimed at the ships at Bassens ('Conger'). Therefore, it is possible that H decided to attach his last two mines to the ships at Bassens, and that the mines found on the pier side of the 'Portland' was from him. Major H also told the 'Crayfish' crew that he had attacked five ships; the damage report only showed three damaged ships in the group at Bordeaux.

The boats 'Catfish' and 'Crayfish returned together all the way to the place which had been the last rest stop of 'Crayfish' on the evening of 11 December. This location was on the river bank above point (G) opposite Bassens.

Major Hasler and Marine Sparks of the 'Catfish' are still at large.

Of the ten saboteurs taking part in the demolition mission seven are definitely either captured or dead. Exact descriptions of the not yet captured crew of 'Catfish' and of Corporal Sheard of the 'Conger' have, after thorough interrogation of those taken prisoner, been given to SD Bordeaux. Information was also given regarding the crossing places of the demarcation line or meeting points used. Further information will be given via general command telex.

Document 9

From: Interrogation Section Dulag Nord Wilhelmshaven
Re: Interrogation of British commandos operating against blockade breakers in Bordeaux 3/1/43

A further deployment of demolition commandos against ships must be expected . . . [See previous signal on] fate of the collapsible boats. During the interrogations it was established that the name of the canoes is painted on the port side in blue paint, and had been painted over in camouflage paint a few days before embarkation in Scotland.

Investigations carried out on 3/1/43 found that the boat mentioned in [previous signal] had drifted ashore some time ago on the Île de Re and had been secured at La Pallice. After the removal of the camouflage paint the name 'Conger' was found. The body of Marine Moffat, who belonged to the crew of the boat, had also been washed ashore on the Île de Re.

On 3/1/43 it was also established that the two canoes secured at Blaye on 12/12/42, which are stored at Bordeaux, have the names 'Crayfish' and 'Catfish'. The name 'Crayfish' could only be deciphered after the careful removal of the camouflage paint. This agrees completely with information found concerning the occurrence under [previous signal]. The above is seen as an important confirmation of the correctness of the reports made by the Interrogation Section Dulag Nord.

Therefore only one canoe i.e. 'Cuttlefish' is outstanding [see previous signal] which drifted ashore at Le Verdon on 8/12/42 but was not recovered.

It is noticeable that the boat 'Catfish' of the leader of the enterprise showed the fewest signs of destruction (the cutting of the boat hull occurred on one side and to a rather small extent) and that none of the boats that had been damaged by cutting did actually sink. The suspicion brought forward by Bordeaux [see previous signal] that the finding of the canoes was not contrary to the intentions of the saboteurs, perhaps to camouflage other aids, cannot be dismissed.

Training in preparation for the enterprise

Under the leadership of Major Hasler two sabotage units (special sections) made up from various parts of the Royal Marines received special training in summer '42 for ship demolition and similar purposes. The unit which was deployed during the night of 7/12/42 was 'Section One', and apart from those named in [previous signal] there was also Colley, who was number 13 and a reserve on the submarine trip. The special training of both units began at the end of July 42 and was as follows for the first unit:

From the end of July until the beginning of October 42. Accommodation in private quarters in Portsmouth, officers separated from other ranks. Boat training with canoes made from rubber, that is the collapsible boat type with keel (not rubber dinghies). Swimming training also carried out, partly with DSEA (Davis Submarine Escape Apparatus), as well as running, climbing and marching. One long march over fifty miles without kit. Some training occurred at night. Officers, especially Major H., took part in everything. Some unsuitable personnel were replaced.

First week of October 42. Short stay in Clyde estuary on board a ship with living accommodation, 'Al Rawdah', which was anchored in Holy Loch. First training with mines and the new canoes, which were used in the operation; these were more fragile than those previous used in Portsmouth which had a wooden floor and no keel. The specialist of the SD already obtained the description of the mines on 10/12/42 when interrogating the crew of 'Coalfish' [see previous signal]. Embarkation of the whole unit with canoes on submarine No. 339; 24-hour sea journey. Practice embarkation and disembarkation of the canoes was carried out three times at sea during night-time, apparently without incident. Security for the operation was tight. The canoes were stored on a lighter, which was anchored about two cable lengths (370m) from the accommodation ship. The crews went to the lighter by lifeboat and started their exercises from there.

Second week of October 42. Return to Portsmouth to the same private quarters and continuation of training. In addition there was service on port protection duties to familiarize the demolition commandos with defensive warfare.

Last week of October 42. Again journey to Holy Loch, Clyde estuary, for continued intense training with the canoes. To get the crews used to genuine situations, the Dutch freighter 'Jan van Gelder', which was also called 'Scambag' by the sailors, was used as a target ship. 'Jan van Gelder' had a Dutch crew in part, and flew the Dutch flag. The ship also served as submarine escort. To simulate the tidal flow the target ship travelled at a speed of 4 to 5 knots, and the commandos attached safe limpets to the ship's side in the prescribed manner, below the waterline. These exercises were also carried out during the night, and in bad weather, allegedly without incident.

The second sabotage unit also consisted of 12 men and was led by First Lieutenant Gordon. Their quarters in Portsmouth were approximately one mile from the quarters of the first unit. Joint exercises did not take place, or if they did, then only rarely, but the two units played football against each other. The interrogation established the following names: Sergeant King, Corporals Bick and Johnson, Marines Stevens, Lambert, Duncan and Watson.

The training in Portsmouth was the same as for 'Section One'. However, a transfer to Scotland for this unit has been denied. When and where the next mission is to take place could not be established, but the mission should be expected in the near future.

Additional Information

During defence exercises the units were briefed as follows by Major Hasler. In future the use of special torpedoes should be expected, which would be steered by two men riding on them. Only the upper bodies of the men would be seen above water. We refer to a report (report number at present not determined) which comes from the interrogation of a sabotage unit captured in Norway, and which was sent to [reference given].

Corporal Laver had previously served on the battleship 'Rodney' [see previous report]. He took part as an ammunition handler for the secondary armament (forward turret, port side) against the

'Bismarck' and confirmed, more or less, last year's report (date and no. at the moment not yet determinable) which resulted from the interrogation of another crewman serving the secondary armament concerning the number of shots fired from the heavy turrets, and the use of the secondary armament. He also stated that towards the end of the battle 'Rodney' had fired all (allegedly 12) torpedoes against 'Bismarck', one of which hit. This reference report is not the interrogation of pilots, which was carried out in Oberusel by the interrogation section of Dulag Nord, but of a naval prisoner who was interrogated in Wilhelmshaven.

Corporal Laver also confirmed in detail an incident involving an unexploded Luftwaffe bomb hit on 'Rodney' off the Norwegian coast. A heavy bomb broke through the three upper decks, beside the 12cm Flak [4-inch AA] position near the forward 15.2cm [6-inch] turret on the port side, and also near the funnel. The bomb broke up and did not penetrate the armoured deck. The nose cone of the bomb was thrown overboard by four men.

Personnel of the interrogation section returned to Paris on Tuesday 5 January. Interrogation officer 'C' is possibly going to return to Bordeaux for clarification of any outstanding details.

Although it is now almost sixty years on, reading these secret documents for the first time sent a shiver down my spine. The Germans, noted for their efficiency, demonstrate a ruthless determination to get at the truth. Although confused at the outset, they gradually built up a picture of our raid, from its conception right through to delivery. I can't believe that our lads disclosed so much, and in particular the mention of our training in Scotland, and the development of the two-man sub. One wonders what other sources of intelligence the Germans had at their disposal.

Had I known, during our escape through occupied territory, that the Germans not only had our names, but also exact descriptions of Major Hasler and myself, it would have added a heavier burden to the one we were already carrying. To think of the close encounter we had with a group of Germans on our way through St Même-les-Carrières, the thought of the enemy being able to recognize us, leaves me cold. I remember, too, how Monsieur DuBois, who sheltered us in those dark days, relieved me of my dog tag, telling me that if I were routinely stopped and searched I would stand a better chance without it. I didn't think too much about it at the time, but later did wonder if I had been wise to give it up. After all, even though dressed in civilian clothes, with my identity disc hanging around my neck I could still have claimed to be a soldier trying to escape. Now I am thinking, 'Did the farmer know that the Germans had our descriptions?' It would certainly explain things. Had I been stopped and searched, the ID disc would have shown without question that I was one of the two they were looking for. My fate would have been sealed. I owe so much to that farmer.

We had dented the enemy's armour, and they bloody well didn't like it. Heads would roll in their own camp, that was for sure; but what they did to our lads was unforgivable.

Index